The Changing Vice-Presidency

The Changing Vice-Presidency

Roy Hoopes

Thomas Y. Crowell   New York

Library of Congress Cataloging in Publication Data

Hoopes, Roy, 1922–
    The changing Vice-Presidency.
    SUMMARY: Through biographical sketches of each
vice-president, traces the evolution of what is now one
of the most important jobs in the United States, with
special focus on recent vice-presidents.
    1. Vice-Presidents—United States—History—Juvenile
literature. 2. Vice-Presidents—United States—
Juvenile literature. [1. Vice-Presidents] I. Title.
JK609.5.H66   1981   353.03'18   [920]   79–8039
ISBN 0–690–03975–1   ISBN 0–690–03976–X (lib. bdg.)

1 2 3 4 5 6 7 8 9 10
FIRST EDITION

420
400

C. 1

ACKNOWLEDGMENTS

I wish to extend my appreciation to Peter Teely, Alexi Reed, and Shirley Green in Vice-President George Bush's office, and to Al Eisele and Ann Stock in former Vice-President Walter F. Mondale's office for the cooperation and assistance they gave me in the preparation of this book. And I wish to thank White House photographers Cynthia Johnson and Robert McNeely for the use of their photographs of Vice-Presidents Bush and Mondale, as well as Billy Shaddix in the Carter White House photography office for his cooperation. Appreciation is also extended to Betty South, in former Senator Muriel Humphrey's office; Richard Holzhausen and Richard McNeil, in the National Archives; Hugh Morrow, in former Vice-President Nelson A. Rockefeller's office; and NBC artist Betty Wells. The archives staff of the Harry S. Truman, Lyndon B. Johnson, and Dwight D. Eisenhower presidential libraries were also extremely helpful in responding to my requests for photographs. I also wish to thank my wife, Cora, for her editorial assistance and my sons, Spencer and Tom, for help with the camera and in the darkroom.

Sources of comments about the vice-presidency included in chapter Six are: Harry S. Truman, *Memoirs;* Lyndon B. Johnson, *The Vantage Point;* Hubert H. Humphrey, "Memorandum to Vice-President Gerald R. Ford"; Gerald R. Ford, *Harpers* Magazine; Walter Mondale, *U.S. News and World Report.*

Contents

The Changing Vice-Presidency

On January 22, 1945, Vice-President Harry S. Truman prepares to bang down the gavel, presiding for the first time over the United States Senate. Three months after this photograph was taken, Truman became president after the death of Franklin D. Roosevelt.   *Associated Press*

1

The Vice-Presidency

The vice-president of the United States is one of the most powerful and important leaders in the nation. His official duties, however, as set forth in the original Constitution, are very few. In fact, only two specific duties are required of the vice-president:

The vice-president of the United States shall be president of the Senate, but shall have no vote, unless they be equally divided.

and

In case of the removal of the president from office, or of his death, resignation, or inability to discharge the powers and duties of the said office, the same shall devolve on the vice-president . . .

In other words, although he presides over the Senate, he does not have a vote unless he is called upon to break a tie. And, he has no official power to lead the country unless he is forced to assume the presidency. As a result, from the earliest days of our country, the office was considered unimportant and a sure way for a public official to disappear into obscurity. John Adams, the country's first vice-president, said it is "the most insignificant office that ever the invention of man contrived."

1

The office was considered so insignificant that, at various times in our history, political scientists and historians have suggested it be abolished. As recently as 1974, historian Arthur Schlesinger, Jr., proposed that the office be eliminated, and if a president died while serving or was incapacitated, a temporary president (perhaps the secretary of state) should lead the country until a special election could be held.

The Vice-Presidency:
Transition Job to Fame—Or Oblivion

There have been forty-three vice-presidents in our history, thirteen of whom have gone from the vice-presidency to the presidency. Nine of them became president as a result of the president's removal from office either by death or resignation. Seven of them—John Tyler, Millard Fillmore, Andrew Johnson, Chester A. Arthur, Theodore Roosevelt, Harry S. Truman, and Gerald R. Ford—served in the vice-presidency less than a year before they were called upon to become president. And perhaps the most famous vice-presidents—Andrew Johnson, Theodore Roosevelt, and Harry S. Truman—were vice-president for only a few months. Their fame came from what happened to them after they became president.

Clearly, throughout most of our history, the vice-presidency was not a job to be sought if you wanted power and fame. The fact that Republican leaders in 1900 thought that the best way to get rid of the pesky Theodore Roosevelt was to offer him the vice-presidency is a good indication of what the nineteenth-century politicians thought of the job. The thirteen vice-presidents we discuss in the following chapter emphasize the point. They only became important once they assumed the presidency.

2

Vice-President Bush greeting Rodney Sickmann, who had been held hostage in Iran, when he arrived in Washington from Wiesbaden.　　*Cynthia Johnson/The White House*

As the principal spokesman for the administration's policies, the modern vice-president spends much of his time on airplanes. He is constantly traveling around the country—to attend meetings, conferences, ceremonies, political rallies, funerals, and, sometimes, even for a little pleasure. Here, Vice-President Walter F. Mondale arrives in Boston to give a speech to the American Federation of Teachers.　　*Robert McNeely/The White House*

Vice-presidential candidate Harry S. Truman (left) discusses political strategy with President Franklin D. Roosevelt at the beginning of the 1944 presidential campaign.

The Harry S. Truman Library

Harry S. Truman went on to be elected president in his own right in 1948, and he chose as his vice-president Senator Alben W. Barkley. Above, the Trumans and the Barkleys return triumphantly to Washington in an open car after their upset victory. In the back seat, President-elect Truman is waving and Vice-President-elect Barkley is on his far left. In the middle is Democratic National Chairman Robert Hannegan. In the front seat are (left to right) Mrs. Truman, Margaret Truman (daughter), and Mrs. Barkley. Truman made certain that Barkley was completely informed about what was going on in the government and ready to take over if anything happened to the president.

The White House

Although it has not always been the case, the vice-president today always meets with the president's cabinet. Above, Vice-President Richard M. Nixon can be seen in the middle, on the left side of the table, across from President Dwight D. Eisenhower. This formal photograph of President Eisenhower's first cabinet was taken early in 1953. From left to right, the cabinet members are: (seated) Henry Cabot Lodge, Douglas McKay, George M. Humphrey, Richard M. Nixon, Herbert Brownell, Jr., Sinclair Weeks, Oveta Culp Hobby, Sherman Adams, Joseph Dodge, Arthur Flemming, Martin P. Durkin, Arthur E. Summerfield, John Foster Dulles, President Eisenhower, Charles E. Wilson, Ezra Taft Benson, Harold Stassen, (standing) Philip Young, Robert Cutler.   *The Dwight D. Eisenhower Library*

Vice-President Lyndon B. Johnson, as head of the National Aeronautics and Space Council, inspects a West Coast space facility.   *The Lyndon B. Johnson Library*

Vice-President Hubert H. Humphrey, whom President Lyndon B. Johnson chose as his running mate in 1964, was also given many official duties, including frequent trips abroad representing the United States. Here, with Mrs. Humphrey, he is greeting a farmer in Ludhiana, India, on a 1968 trip to Asia.   *United States Information Service*

Vice-President Spiro T. Agnew (left) was used extensively by President Richard M. Nixon for political speeches and attacks. This was a task Nixon, as vice-president, performed for President Eisenhower, which led to Agnew's sometimes being called "Nixon's Nixon."   *The White House*

After being in the vice-presidency less than a year, Gerald R. Ford became president when President Richard M. Nixon was forced to resign because of the Watergate scandals. In this photo, Ford speaks with members of the Washington press corps shortly after Nixon's resignation. *The National Archives*

"I never wanted to be vice-president of anything," said Nelson A. Rockefeller (enroute to Salem, West Virginia, to give the graduation address at Salem College). Nevertheless, he accepted the vice-presidency when it was offered to him by President Gerald R. Ford. *Jack Kightlinger*

However, most students of government would probably not agree with Schlesinger. The vice-presidency is no longer considered an insignificant office. Since that dramatic day in April 1945, when Harry S. Truman was suddenly thrust into the White House after the death of President Franklin D. Roosevelt, the concept of the job has gradually changed. With few exceptions, the men who have held the office were carefully selected by the presidential candidates as men who might someday succeed them.

Recent vice-presidents have been given more and more responsibilities in preparation for the time when they might have to assume the powers of the presidency. And none too soon: three of the six vice-presidents from Alben W. Barkley to Gerald R. Ford eventually became president. And two of these, like Truman, were called into office suddenly because of an unexpected crisis.

As a result, the office of the vice-presidency has finally come into its own after years of ridicule and neglect. Historians and commentators no longer make fun of it, and voters are also giving more serious thought to the men they vote for as vice-president. As the late Senator Hubert H. Humphrey, once vice-president himself, said, the vice-presidency is not only needed, "it is necessary. It has contributed significantly to the nation." And if the office continues to evolve, as it has in recent years, its contribution will increase.

Vice-President Walter F. Mondale studies a document with President Jimmy Carter.

Robert McNeely/The White House

Vice-President Lyndon B. Johnson being sworn in as president on *Air Force One* in Dallas, Texas, immediately after the assassination of President John F. Kennedy. Mrs. Johnson is to his right and Mrs. Kennedy is to his left.

2

Under Which President
Did Theodore Roosevelt Serve?

From the earliest days of the nation, men who have served as vice-president of the United States have become famous only if they succeeded to the presidency or achieved fame in some other capacity. As a result, when you think of a man who was both vice-president and president, you usually remember him as president.

The men discussed in this chapter have all been president. But before that they were vice-president—although most people would not remember this fact, or know under which president each served. As Woodrow Wilson said in 1885, in his book *Congressional Government,* "There is very little to be said about the vice-president. . . . His importance consists in the fact that he may cease to be vice-president."

John Adams, 1789–1797

John Adams, the country's first vice-president, served two terms under George Washington before succeeding him as our second president. He was born in what is now Quincy, Massachusetts, and grew up on his father's farm. He graduated from Harvard in 1755 and went into law, eventually becoming a very successful lawyer. In 1764, he married Abigail Smith, and with their three sons and two daughters, the Adamses became one of the most famous and important families in the nation's history.

Adams was drawn into revolutionary politics when he opposed the Stamp Act, by which the British attempted to tax the colonists, even though the Americans had no representation in the British Parliament. He was a delegate to both the First and Second Continental Congresses, where he distinguished himself for his moderate but forceful views. He was sent to Europe as a diplomat, representing our young nation in France, the Netherlands, and England. Later, he negotiated the Treaty of Paris, which ended the revolutionary war.

Adams did not sign the Declaration of Independence because he was still in England at the time of the signing. But he returned home in time to take an active part in forming a government; and in the country's first election, in 1888, he and George Washington were both candidates for president. Washington received more votes in the electoral college and Adams received the next highest number. So, under the system for choosing our presidents and vice-presidents then in force (see chapter 4), Adams became vice-president. Adams was hardworking and loyal. At first he tended to lecture the senators over whom he presided, but this inspired so much criticism that he gradually became less vocal in the Senate. He did, however, cast twenty-nine tie-breaking votes, a record that stands to this day.

When party politics began to emerge during Washington's presidency, Adams became the leader of the Federalists. His principal opponent was Thomas Jefferson, leader of the Democratic-Republicans, the forerunner of the present-day Democratic party. When Washington announced that he would not seek a third term, Adams was his party's natural choice for president, and Jefferson was the candidate of the Democratic-Republican party. Adams was elected president in 1796, but was defeated four years later by Jefferson. He retired to his Massachusetts home and lived to see his son, John Quincy Adams, elected president in 1824. Two years later, he died at the age of ninety.

Thomas Jefferson, 1797–1801

Our second vice-president was one of the young country's most brilliant and distinguished leaders. Thomas Jefferson was born in the town of Shadwell, in what today is known as Albemarle County, Virginia, in 1743. At age sixteen, he entered William and Mary College, at Williamsburg, and graduated in 1762. Jefferson was elected to the Virginia House of Burgesses and early in his career became active in the opposition to British parliamentary rule in the colonies. He took a leading part in the Continental Congress, and after the revolutionary war began, he was appointed member of a commission to draft the Declaration of Independence. The final draft, the document which is so often quoted today, was written almost solely by Jefferson.

After the war, Jefferson was governor of Virginia, a member of the United States Congress, minister to France, and secretary of state. During Washington's second term, he retired to his home at Monticello, but as leader of the developing Democratic-Republican party, he was soon drawn back into politics. He ran against John Adams, the Federalist, in 1796, and received sixty-eight electoral votes to Adams's seventy-one. Under the electoral system used then, Jefferson became Adams's vice-president, even though they were members of opposing political parties.

Jefferson's experiences in presiding over the Senate prompted him to write his famous *Manual of Parliamentary Practice,* which is still used today. He was also a leader in the opposition to the Alien and Sedition Acts of 1798, which deprived the country of freedom of speech and the press.

In 1800, Jefferson was elected president after a very complex situation developed in the electoral college (see chapter 4), and Aaron Burr became his vice-president. Jefferson served as president from 1801 to 1809. One of the highlights of his administration was the purchase of the Louisiana Territory from France, which gave the country what eventually became most of its midwestern states.

After his presidency, Jefferson returned to Monticello to devote the rest of his life to his many interests—music, architecture, philosophy, religion, law, and education. During this period, he planned and founded the University of Virginia, climaxing one of the most distinguished careers in American history.

Martin Van Buren, 1833–1837

Martin Van Buren was born in Kinderhook, New York, in 1782. He grew up on a farm and began studying law at the age of fourteen. He continued studying law in New York City and then returned to Kinderhook in 1803 to pass the bar exam and begin his own practice.

In 1812, he was elected to the state senate and four years later was appointed New York's attorney general. A Democrat, Van Buren showed considerable skill as a party leader and organizer and served as a U.S. senator from 1821 to 1828. He then was elected governor of New York, but served only two months before resigning to become secretary of state under newly elected President Andrew Jackson. By helping Jackson politically in a number of ways—especially in Jackson's feud with Senator John C. Calhoun—he earned the president's staunch support. When the Senate defeated Jackson's attempt to make Van Buren minister to Great Britain, Jackson picked Van Buren as his vice-presidential running mate in the election of 1832. As vice-president, Van Buren supported Jackson in his famous fight with the Bank of the United States, and debates in the Senate became increasingly bitter. For a time there were rumors of a plot to assassinate Van Buren, so the vice-president carried two loaded pistols as he presided over the Senate.

With President Jackson's backing, Van Buren was nominated as the Democratic party's presidential candidate in 1836. He easily defeated William Henry Harrison, but his administration was hampered by many problems inherited from the Jackson administration. Van Buren also had to cope with the nation's first serious depression, brought on by the panic of 1837, in which thousands of Americans were financially ruined. Van Buren was defeated for the presidency in 1840 and retired to his New York estate, Lindenwald, where he remained active in politics for the next twenty years. In 1848, he was a candidate for the presidency on the antislavery Free-Soil party ticket, and lost. But he took so many votes from the Democrat, Lewis Cass, that the Whig party candidate, Zachary Taylor, won.

John Tyler, 1841

John Tyler was vice-president of the United States for less time than any man in history—one month.

Tyler was born on his father's estate in Charles City County, Virginia, in 1790. His father was a governor of Virginia, Speaker of the Virginia House of Delegates, and a judge. He attended William and Mary College, where he studied politics, wrote poetry, and played the violin. He graduated at the age of seventeen, then studied law under his father. He was admitted to the Virginia bar in 1809 and was elected to the Virginia House of Delegates at the age of twenty-one. In 1813, he ran for a vacant seat in the U.S. House of Representatives and won. When he was thirty-one, he ran for the U.S. Senate and lost. He served briefly as chancellor of William and Mary College before being elected governor of Virginia in 1825. In 1827, he ran for the Senate again and won. But he voted against the "Force Bill," which would give President Jackson the power to use the army and the navy to support the laws of the land—specifically to force South Carolina to obey the tariff laws. Tyler did not back South Carolina's defiance of the federal government, but he was opposed to using federal force against any state. When the Virginia state legislature ordered Senator Tyler to support Jackson, he resigned.

In 1840, hoping to win Democratic votes, the Federalists chose Tyler to run as the vice-presidential candidate with William Henry Harrison, the hero of the battle of Tippecanoe. Tyler, by this time a disenchanted Democrat, accepted, and won in an election campaign famous for the slogan "Tippecanoe and Tyler Too."

President Harrison died one month after coming into office, and Tyler became president. He quickly came into opposition with William Henry Harrison's Whig party, which was now led by Senator Henry Clay. Tyler's Whig cabinet eventually resigned in protest against his policies and Tyler was in the rather unusual position of being a president without a party. He led the country in this confused situation for four years. Historians consider that his most important achievement in office was action that eventually led to the annexation of Texas to the Union.

After he left office, Tyler retired to his estate in Virginia. In 1861, he was appointed to lead a peace commission to Washington, which hoped to resolve the issues threatening to divide the Union. The mission was unsuccessful. When the Civil War began, Tyler was elected to the Confederate House of Representatives, but he died in 1862, before he could take office.

Millard Fillmore, 1849–1850

Even though he became president after Zachary Taylor died, Millard Fillmore is still virtually unknown in American history. He was born on a farm in western New York in 1800. He did not have a formal education, but he studied law in his spare time and was admitted to the New York bar in 1823. He began to practice law in East Aurora,

New York, and soon gained a reputation as one of the state's most able lawyers. In 1828, he was elected to the New York State legislature as a protégé of Thurlow Weed, one of New York's most powerful political bosses. In 1832, he was elected to the U.S. House of Representatives and soon became prominent in Washington as the chairman of the powerful House Ways and Means Committee, which controlled the nation's spending. In 1844, the Whigs considered Fillmore a candidate for the vice-presidency, but he chose to run instead for governor of New York. He was defeated, and four years later he was chosen as vice-presidential candidate on the Whig ticket with General Zachary Taylor and won.

The year after he took office, Taylor died from fever and Millard Fillmore became president. In his short time in office, he supported and then signed the Compromise of 1850, which helped prevent civil war for ten years. In 1852, the Whigs nominated General Winfield Scott, and Fillmore drifted into obscurity, emerging as the leader of the "Know-Nothing" party, officially called the American party, opposed to the German and Irish immigrants. It was conducted like a secret society, and whenever its members were asked what the party's principals were, they were instructed to answer: "I know nothing." In 1856, the Whigs and the Know-Nothings nominated Fillmore for president, but he was defeated by Democrat James Buchanan. He retired from politics to practice law in Buffalo and died in 1874 at the age of seventy-four.

Andrew Johnson, 1865

Andrew Johnson was vice-president of the United States for less than forty-five days. But he will always be famous in history as the man who came into office after the assassination of President Abraham Lincoln and as the only president the Senate tried to impeach.

Andrew Johnson was born in Raleigh, North Carolina, in 1808. His father died when he was three and his family was too poor for young Andy to go to school. He had to work, and at age fourteen was apprenticed to a tailor. When his family moved to east Tennessee, Johnson opened his own tailor shop. He learned to read in his spare time, and his wife, Eliza McCardle, taught him to write.

Like fellow Tennessean Andrew Jackson, Johnson was a great believer in the common man. He was opposed to the powerful landowners who dominated Tennessee, and he eventually became interested in politics as a way to advance the interests of the small landowners and tradesmen. In 1828, the year Andrew Jackson was elected president, Johnson was elected alderman of Greeneville, Tennessee, and two years later, mayor. In following years he served in the Tennessee House of Representatives; the state senate; and the U.S. House of Representatives, where he tried to take a middle ground on the issue of slavery, which dominated national concern. He was governor of Tennessee from 1853 to 1857 and then became a member of the U.S. Senate. Although he supported slavery and was opposed to abolition, the preservation of the Union was important to him and he was against secession. When Tennessee seceded from the Union, he denounced the secessionists as traitors and was the only southerner who remained in the Senate. In 1862, when Union forces won control of Tennessee, Lincoln appointed Johnson military governor of the state. He was an effective and enlightened leader during a difficult period.

Johnson became the most prominent of the so-called War Democrats. This group joined the Republicans to form the National Union party, which nominated Abraham Lincoln for a second term and picked Andrew Johnson as Lincoln's running mate. Less than forty-five days after he took office, Lincoln was assassinated and Andrew Johnson became president. Johnson's conciliatory policies toward the South quickly brought him into conflict with the radical Republicans, who controlled the Senate after the congressional elections of 1866. In 1868, they resolved to impeach him. The trial began in March and lasted more than two months and then the Senate voted and failed to impeach Johnson by one vote.

Johnson had hoped the Democrats would renominate him in 1868, but the party chose, instead, Governor Horatio Seymour of New York, who was defeated by Civil War hero General Ulysses S. Grant. Johnson's last important act in the White House was a Christmas Proclamation in 1868 pardoning all southerners who had taken part in the Civil War. In 1874, Johnson was again elected to the Senate, but he attended only one short session before he died in Tennessee in 1875.

Chester A. Arthur, 1881

Chester A. Arthur was another vice-president to serve for less than a year in office. He was born in Fairfield, Vermont, in 1830. He attended upstate New York public schools, then entered Union College, from which he graduated with honors in 1848. After teaching school for a brief period, he studied law and he was admitted to the New York bar in 1854.

During the Civil War, Arthur held several administrative posts in the state of New York, and he became known as a loyal member of the "Tweed gang" in New York City. President Ulysses S. Grant appointed him collector of the port of New York, where he gained a reputation for honesty and for rewarding New York's political workers. At the Republican convention of 1880, the party nominated James A. Garfield as their presidential candidate. The "stalwarts" as the supporters of ex-President Grant were known, backed their man. In order to unite the party and appease the stalwarts, the Republicans nominated one of Grant's supporters—Chester A. Arthur—as their vice-presidential candidate.

The Republicans were elected, but less than four months after he was inaugurated, Garfield was assassinated by a disappointed office-seeker.

As a member of the stalwarts and one who favored the spoils system in government, Arthur had a difficult time in the presidency. The people had grown tired of the political corruption following the Civil War and the spirit of reform was in the air. However, Arthur surprised everyone by being a better president than most expected. The first major Civil Service Reform Act was passed in his administration. Arther was not renominated at the Republican Convention in 1884 and he subsequently retired from politics. He died in 1886.

Theodore Roosevelt, 1901

Theodore Roosevelt, who was president from 1901 to 1909, was one of the most colorful and famous men in American history. But few people remember that he served as vice-president for six months in 1901 under William McKinley.

Roosevelt was born in New York City in 1858. As a boy, he had asthma, was not very strong, and was nearsighted, which forced him to wear glasses from the age of twelve. To overcome his weaknesses, his father built a gymnasium and "Teddy" worked hard to develop as a strong and courageous young man. He graduated from Harvard in 1880 and went on to study law at Columbia University. While a student he was elected as a Republican to the New York State legislature in 1881 for three consecutive years.

In 1884, he suffered a double tragedy: on the same day, his wife died in childbirth and his mother from typhoid fever. Roosevelt gave up politics and moved to his cattle ranches in the Dakota Territory. He hoped the hard life of a cowboy would help him recover from his sorrow. He also began writing books, which he continued to do the rest of his life. When a snowstorm destroyed most of his cattle, in 1886, Roosevelt returned to New York, where Republican leaders persuaded him to run for mayor. He was badly defeated. In 1888,

Roosevelt campaigned for Republican presidential candidate Benjamin Harrison, and when Harrison won, he rewarded Roosevelt by appointing him director of the Civil Service Commission. He did such a good job that he was reappointed to the position by Democratic President Grover Cleveland in 1893. Two years later, friends asked whether he was interested in being a candidate for president and Roosevelt replied: "Don't put such ideas into my head. Every young man wants to be president. But I won't let myself think of it. If I do, I'll be calculating and cautious, and so I'll beat myself. . . . "

Roosevelt campaigned for William McKinley in 1896, and when McKinley won he asked him for a Washington job. McKinley did not especially want the volatile and outspoken young Roosevelt in his administration, but Roosevelt's friends persisted and he was made assistant secretary of the navy.

He believed sea power was the key to national strength and he spent his years in office building up the U.S. Navy. In 1898, when the United States declared war on Spain after the battleship *Maine* was sunk at Havana, Roosevelt resigned his post and formed a cavalry unit to fight in Cuba. They were known as the "Rough Riders," and Roosevelt became famous after he led a victorious charge at San Juan Hill.

Roosevelt returned to America a hero and was soon back in politics. The Republicans faced defeat in the state of New York because of scandals and corruption, and although the party leaders did not like Roosevelt, they thought his reputation and war record might save the party. So they agreed to let him run for governor, and he won.

Roosevelt was gaining a reputation as a strong, independent political figure, and he demonstrated that he was not sympathetic to the business interests that dominated the Republican party. And as governor of the most powerful state in the Union, he was emerging as a strong candidate for president in 1904, after William McKinley's second term. So the Republican leaders opposed to Roosevelt figured they had the

President Theodore Roosevelt inspecting construction equipment at the Panama Canal in 1906.

Underwood and Underwood/Library of Congress

perfect solution: they would nominate him for vice-president under McKinley, which would take him out of the politically powerful job of governor of New York and put him in the meaningless, obscure job of vice-president of the United States. Roosevelt knew what was happening and was not enthusiastic, but he agreed to go along for the good of the party. However, the plan backfired on the Republican leaders. Six months after his inauguration for his second term, President McKinley was assassinated at the opening ceremonies of the Pan American Exposition in Buffalo, New York, and Roosevelt became president. He had spent only four days in March presiding over the Senate as vice-president. Then the Senate adjourned until December and Roosevelt went to Long Island, where he remained until McKinley's death.

As president, Roosevelt, reacting to public anger, took action against many of the nation's biggest and best-known corporations. In forty-three anti-trust suits, he went after the big industries, including J. P. Morgan's railroads, John D. Rockefeller's oil industry, and James B. Duke's tobacco company. As a result, he became famous as a "trust buster." He also developed what many said was an imperialist foreign policy, which, among other things, resulted in America building the Panama Canal.

Roosevelt had pledged he would not run for a third term, but to make certain that his progressive policies were carried out, he engineered the nomination and election of William Howard Taft in 1908. After leaving the White House, he went to Africa on a hunting expedition. When he returned to the United States in 1910, he found the Republican party badly split, with the progressives saying that President Taft had betrayed them. Roosevelt campaigned for the Republican nomination in 1912, but Taft and the conservatives controlled the convention and Taft was renominated. Roosevelt bolted the Republican party, formed the "Bull Moose" party and ran for president. He was not successful, but he did split the Republicans enough to help elect the Democrat, Woodrow Wilson, president. During the campaign, a saloon keeper attempted to assassinate Roosevelt, but he was saved, apparently, by the glass case which he carried in his pocket.

Roosevelt was not active in politics during World War I, but he was a serious candidate for the Republican nomination in 1920. He would have been only sixty-two. But in 1919 he died suddenly of a blood clot in the heart, ending one of the most distinguished careers in American political history.

Calvin Coolidge, 1921–1923

Calvin Coolidge was born in 1872 at Plymouth, Vermont. He attended private schools in Vermont, then entered Amherst College, graduating in 1895. Establishing a law practice in Northampton, Massachusetts, he was elected councilman and then mayor. He was a Republican but not known as an inspirational leader or persuasive speaker. However, he did follow a conventional political career in which he gained a reputation for competence and adherence to party principles. He served in the Massachusetts state senate, was lieutenant governor and finally governor. In office, he gained a national reputation for his handling of the Boston police strike in 1919, which he ended by using the state militia.

At the Republican convention in 1920, Coolidge had considerable support for the presidential nomination, which was won by Senator Warren G. Harding of Ohio. Harding was the choice of the political bosses, who picked him in a "smoke-filled room," a phrase that became famous in political history. To protest against the bosses' dictating the choice of the presidential nominee, the convention picked Coolidge as the vice-presidential candidate. Harding and Coolidge were elected by a substantial margin.

Coolidge was an active vice-president, consulting with the president and giving his advice on policies and appointments. He broke established precedent by attending President Harding's cabinet meetings. He also managed to maintain his reputation for honesty and integrity despite the scandals that dominated the Harding administration. When Harding died in 1923, Coolidge became president—and was re-elected on his own in 1924.

Coolidge's personal honesty and plain-folks sincerity appealed to the American people, who had been shocked by the scandals of the preceding administration. Coolidge was pro-business and his famous statement "The business of America is business" summed up his philosophy and the mood of the American people. His policies, as president, supported big business and his statements also encouraged the stock market speculation which led to the financial crash of 1929. Coolidge announced that he would not seek re-election in 1928, and the Republicans nominated Herbert Hoover, who was elected president.

Coolidge returned to Northampton to write magazine articles, a newspaper column, and his *Autobiography.* He died in 1933.

Harry S. Truman, 1945

Like most of the vice-presidents suddenly called upon to assume the leadership of our country, Harry S. Truman spent a brief time— eighty-three days to be exact—in the vice-presidency. But no man in our history faced the enormous challenges confronting Truman in 1945—the conclusion of the war against Germany and Japan, the decision whether or not to drop the atomic bomb on Japan, and the organization of the United Nations.

Harry S. Truman was born in Lamar, Missouri, in 1884. He went to public schools in Independence, and because he had to wear glasses and was warned by his doctor about injuring his eyes, he was afraid to enter into the usual boyhood games. As a result, he spent his spare time reading, and by the age of fourteen he had read most of the books in the public library. He wanted to go to the U.S. Military Academy at West Point but his eyesight was not good enough. So after he graduated from high school in 1901, he held a number of odd jobs—with the Santa Fe Railroad, the *Kansas City Star* and two Kansas City banks. He also was a member of the Missouri National Guard. When the U.S. became involved in World War I, Truman helped organize a field artillery regiment. He served as commander of an artillery battery in France and was discharged in 1919 with the rank of captain. After the war, he and a friend started a men's clothing store in Kansas City, but the store failed in the depression of the early 1920s. It took Truman fifteen years to pay back his debts.

When the store failed, Truman decided to enter politics. "Big Tom" Pendergast, the party boss in Missouri, thought Truman could win elections because of his war record, farm background, and friendly personality. Despite the fact that he did not graduate from college and attended the Kansas City School of Law only two years, Truman ran for county judge in 1922. He was elected, then defeated in 1924, but re-elected in 1926. He served as county judge until 1934, when Pendergast decided Truman should run for the U.S. Senate. He won, and one of his first assignments was to the Interstate Commerce Committee. When a committee investigation found evidence of vote fraud and financial corruption in the Pendergast machine, Pendergast himself pleaded guilty to income tax evasion. As a result, Pendergast and many of Truman's political friends went to jail, but Truman was never implicated in any of the scandals.

In 1940, although not at war, the nation was spending millions of dollars developing its military preparedness and aiding Britain and France. Early in 1941, the Senate established a committee to investigate the National Defense Program and appointed Senator Truman as its chairman. The Truman Committee, as it quickly became known, found considerable waste and inefficiency in the program, which saved the government millions of dollars.

As a result, by 1944, Truman was a national figure with a reputation for efficient and honest government. At the Democratic National Convention that year, a serious fight developed over the choice of the vice-presidential candidate. It was thought that President Franklin D. Roosevelt, obviously exhausted from the strains of war, might not live out his fourth term. The popular choices for the vice-presidency were Vice-President Henry Wallace, Supreme Court Justice William O. Douglas, and James F. Byrnes, a former South Carolina senator and director of war mobilization. When it became obvious, however, that a fight by these men for the vice-presidency would split the party, Robert Hannegan, chairman of the Democratic National Committee, proposed Truman as a compromise, and Roosevelt accepted. Roosevelt won his fourth term as president and Truman became vice-president. In his eighty-three days in office, he was involved in one historic event: As president of the Senate, he cast a tie-breaking vote that continued America's lend-lease aid to the Allies.

In his first term as president, in addition to his decisions concerning the atomic bomb, waging war against Germany and Japan, and the creation of the United Nations, Truman also promulgated what came to be known as the Truman Doctrine, which guaranteed American aid to any free country that resisted Communist aggression and propaganda. He waged cold war against Russia, by launching the Marshall Plan with American aid, and helped bring about the postwar economic recovery of Europe. At home, he continued Roosevelt's New Deal with policies of his own, which came to be known as the Fair Deal.

Despite his reforms, by 1948 the Republicans seemed certain of victory. Truman had failed to win the confidence of the American people, and when the Democratic party renominated Truman at its

Two months after becoming president, Harry S. Truman (center) meets with British Prime Minister Winston Churchill (left) and Russian Premier Joseph Stalin (right) at the Potsdam Conference.   *U.S. Navy/The Harry S. Truman Library*

convention, one group of Democrats split with the party to form the Progressive party, which supported former Vice-President Henry Wallace for president. Another group split to form the Dixiecrats, who supported South Carolina Governor J. Strom Thurmond. Despite the Democratic party split, Truman narrowly defeated Republican candidate Thomas E. Dewey in one of the most dramatic upsets in the history of the presidency.

Truman's second term was overshadowed by the Korean War and the attacks on his administration by Senator Joseph R. McCarthy, who accused the Truman government of sympathy toward the Communists—despite the fact that Truman was actively resisting Communist expansion in Europe and Asia. Truman decided to retire from politics in 1952, although he campaigned actively for the Democratic candidate, Adlai Stevenson. After Stevenson's defeat, Truman retired to Independence, Missouri, where he died in 1972.

Richard M. Nixon, 1953–1961

Of all the vice-presidents who subsequently became president, only Richard M. Nixon and John Adams—the nation's first vice-president—served two complete terms in the vice-presidency.

Richard M. Nixon was born in Yorba Linda, California, in 1913. He attended public schools in Whittier, California, and graduated from Whittier College in 1934. He went to Duke University on a scholarship to study law, and after his graduation in 1937, he returned to Whittier where he practiced law for five years. In 1942, he worked as an attorney in the Office of Price Administration in Washington, then was commissioned in the navy with the rank of lieutenant.

After the war, in 1946, a committee of California Republicans asked him to run for Congress from the 12th Congressional District. He won and was re-elected in 1948. As a member of the House Un-American Activities Committee, Nixon gained nationwide fame for his role in the Alger Hiss case. Against the opposition of some members of the committee who wanted to drop the case, Nixon persisted and Hiss was eventually convicted of perjury in 1950. The same year, Nixon ran for the Senate from California and won.

Nixon served in the Senate for only two years, but during that time he enhanced his reputation as an anti-Communist crusader. This helped lead to his nomination as Republican vice-presidential candidate in 1952 to campaign with World War II hero General Dwight D. Eisenhower. They defeated Adlai Stevenson and the Democrats, and, in 1953, Nixon began eight years in the vice-presidency.

Nixon was almost dropped from the ticket in 1952, when it was discovered that a "secret fund" had been set up for him by his California admirers when he was in the Congress. But Nixon went on television, and, in his famous "Checkers speech," convinced both the American people and General Eisenhower that he should remain on the Republican ticket.

Encouraged by Eisenhower, Nixon became a very active vice-president. And during three illnesses suffered by Eisenhower while he was in office, Vice-President Nixon filled in for the president. Perhaps the most noteworthy incident that occurred during Nixon's vice-presidency was the attack on him and his wife by an angry mob while they were on a state visit to Venezuela in 1958. By 1960, after eight years as Eisenhower's vice-president, Nixon was the second most powerful man in the Republican party and was easily nominated for the presidency. He was defeated by the Democratic senator from Massachusetts, John F. Kennedy.

In 1962, Nixon made an unsuccessful effort to become governor of California, and when he was defeated, he announced his retirement from politics. However, after practicing law for several years in New York, he returned to politics in 1968 and was nominated Republican candidate for the presidency. He chose Spiro T. Agnew, governor of Maryland, as his running mate, and they defeated Hubert H. Humphrey and Edmund Muskie in a campaign dominated by the public's dissatisfaction with America's military involvement in Vietnam. Nixon promised peace with honor in Vietnam and he and Agnew were elected.

Nixon's first term was marked by economic troubles at home and the difficulty of extricating American troops honorably from Vietnam. He finally achieved a cease-fire in Vietnam, and the recession and inflation plaguing the economy were not enough to prevent his re-

President Nixon (left) discusses foreign policy with his secretary of state, Henry Kissinger, in 1972.   *The White House*

election. In fact, he and Agnew won a landslide victory over Democratic Senator George McGovern in 1972.

However, Nixon's second term brought total disaster for Nixon, Agnew, and the Republican party. During the campaign of 1972, seven men were caught trying to break into the headquarters of the Democratic National Committee in the Watergate Office Building. It developed that the men were working for the Committee for the Re-election of the President. Not enough information about CREEP's involvement with the break-in came out in 1972 to prevent Nixon's re-election, but, by early 1973, it was apparent that many top men in the Nixon White House staff were involved in the Watergate affair. An attempt was made to "cover up" the extent to which the White House was involved, and, in the process, the president's men violated the law. In addition, several other scandals involving campaign financing rocked the administration, and Nixon's vice-president, Spiro Agnew, was forced to resign after pleading guilty (actually, "no contest") to charges of illegal financial transactions while he had been governor of Maryland. Nixon appointed House Minority Leader Gerald Ford to replace Agnew as vice-president.

As the Watergate case began to unfold, it was revealed that Nixon was secretly recording most of the conversations that took place in the Oval Office. A legal battle developed over ownership of the tapes. On July 24, 1974, the Supreme Court ruled, eight to zero, that Nixon must surrender the tapes to the Watergate special prosecutor, and Nixon was doomed because the tapes revealed information that indicated his involvement in the Watergate cover-up. The House of Representatives recommended impeachment of the president, but, before impeachment proceedings could be initiated, President Nixon resigned, becoming the first president in history to resign from his office. On August 9, 1974, Vice-President Gerald Ford became president of the United States. He appointed Nelson A. Rockefeller as his vice-president.

Lyndon B. Johnson, 1961–1963

Senator Lyndon Baines Johnson of Texas tried hard to win the Democratic presidential nomination in 1960 but lost it to Senator John F. Kennedy of Massachusetts. When Kennedy offered him the vice-presidential nomination, many of Johnson's friends said he should not accept it. Young Kennedy would probably be in office eight years, it was argued, and the vice-presidency would surely mark the end of Johnson's effective political career. He accepted the nomination, however, and two and a half years after his inauguration, he was dramatically thrust into the presidency by the assassination of President John F. Kennedy in Dallas.

Lyndon B. Johnson was born on a farm in central Texas in 1908. His father, Samuel E. Johnson, was a schoolteacher and a farmer who served five years in the Texas House of Representatives. When Lyndon was five, his family moved to Johnson City, founded by his grandfather. After graduating from high school at the age of fifteen, he decided he did not want to go to college. However, he changed his mind after hitchhiking around the country and holding a series of odd jobs. In 1927, he entered Texas State Teachers College, and, after graduation, taught public speaking at a high school in Houston.

In 1931, Johnson became active in politics, helping Richard M. Kleberg, Sr., a Democrat, campaign in a special election for a seat in the U.S. House of Representatives. When Kleberg won, he took young Johnson to Washington with him as his secretary.

In 1935, President Franklin D. Roosevelt appointed Johnson head of the Texas branch of the National Youth Administration, a job that helped the twenty-six-year-old Johnson become popular and well known in his state. Two years later, Johnson quit his NYA post and ran for Congress in a special election. He was an avid Roosevelt supporter, even backing Roosevelt's effort to "pack" the Supreme Court with six additional justices in an effort to win Court support for his New Deal legislation. After Johnson won the election and went back to Washington, he and Roosevelt became close friends. In 1938, he was elected to his first full term in the House.

Johnson won re-election in 1940, but was defeated in an attempt to win a Senate seat in a special election in 1941. After the Japanese attacked Pearl Harbor in December of 1941, Johnson went on active military duty in the navy and he was soon being used by President Roosevelt as a special representative in the Pacific. He won a Silver

President Johnson (elbow on table) meets with his military advisers at the LBJ ranch in Texas to discuss the Vietnam War.   *Y. R. Okamoto/The Lyndon B. Johnson Library*

Star when a bomber he was in was attacked by Japanese fighter planes.

In 1943, while he was still at war, friends entered his name in the contest for his House seat and Johnson was re-elected easily. Before the election, Roosevelt had ordered all members of Congress in the armed forces to return to Washington and their jobs, so Johnson came back.

In 1948, Johnson entered the race for a seat in the U.S. Senate and won a run-off election with his primary opponent by eighty-seven votes, which gained him the nickname "Landslide Lyndon." He went on to win the general election easily, and then distinguished himself as his party's "whip" or minority leader. In 1955, he was elected majority leader. He quickly gained a reputation for being one of the most clever and gifted legislative leaders in the history of the Senate.

Johnson was a candidate for the Democratic presidential nomination in 1960, but the convention chose John F. Kennedy. Kennedy picked Johnson as his running mate and they beat Richard M. Nixon and Henry Cabot Lodge in the November elections.

Johnson soon became one of the most active vice-presidents in his-

44

tory, symbolizing the gradual change taking place in the office. He served as chairman of the National Aeronautics and Space Council, the Peace Corps Advisory Council, the President's Committee on Equal Employment Opportunity and on the National Security Council before tragedy suddenly made him president. On November 22, 1963, President Kennedy was assassinated while in a motorcade driving through Dallas. Johnson was riding two cars behind the president when the shots were fired. A Secret Service agent shoved the vice-president to the floor of the car and shielded Johnson with his body. Less than two hours later, the president was dead and Johnson was sworn in as president aboard *Air Force One,* the president's plane.

Johnson was credited with an excellent job of governing the nation in the difficult transition days after President Kennedy's assassination. In 1964, he chose Hubert H. Humphrey as his vice-presidential running mate, and they beat Republican presidential candidate Barry Goldwater in a landslide election.

Johnson's years as president were marred by the tragic war in Vietnam and the violence resulting from protests against the war and the explosive civil rights movement. At home, Johnson pushed through Congress a massive domestic legislative program, which became the foundation for the "Great Society." But abroad, he could not win a victory in Vietnam or bring about an honorable U.S. withdrawal, and the country eventually turned against him. As the 1968 presidential campaign drew near, with Democratic Senator Eugene McCarthy receiving an impressive 42.4 percent of the vote in the New Hampshire primary and New York Senator Robert F. Kennedy (President Kennedy's brother) entering the race, Johnson announced his intention to retire at the end of his term. Humphrey was nominated by the Democrats and he and his running mate, Senator Edmund Muskie of Maine, were defeated by Richard M. Nixon and Spiro Agnew.

After Nixon's inauguration, Johnson retired to his farm in Texas where he died in 1973.

Gerald R. Ford, 1973–1974

Gerald R. Ford was the first vice-president to be selected under the provisions of the Twenty-fifth Amendment to the Constitution, which determines what happens when a President is ill, dies in office, or is forced to resign. He was selected by President Nixon and the

Congress, which makes him the only vice-president who did not have a vote cast for him by the American people.

Gerald R. Ford was born in Omaha, Nebraska, in 1913. His family moved to Grand Rapids, Michigan, where he attended school. In 1931, he entered the University of Michigan, where he was the star of a championship football team. In 1934, he was named Michigan's most valuable player. After college, he entered Yale Law School and when he graduated he returned to Michigan where he was admitted to the bar in 1941. He practiced law for a short time in Michigan and then entered the navy as a physical fitness training officer. Later, he shifted to gunnery and eventually saw service in the Pacific on the aircraft carrier U.S.S. *Monterey*.

After the war, Ford resumed his law practice in Grand Rapids and went into politics. He was elected to Congress in 1948, after upsetting the incumbent Republican congressman, Bartel Jonkman, in the primary elections. In Congress, Ford decided that the second most powerful job in Washington was not the vice-presidency but Speaker of the House. A career in the House became his ambition, and he worked hard at being a good representative and a loyal Republican. He supported the Republican leadership on almost every major bill, and was re-elected for twelve consecutive terms.

In 1973, when Vice-President Spiro Agnew was forced to resign, President Nixon picked Congressman Ford to replace him, and his selection was endorsed by the House 387 to 35, and by the Senate 92 to 3.

During the congressional hearings on Ford's confirmation, it was evident that most members of Congress thought they were passing judgment on the next president of the United States. Already it was felt that President Nixon would not complete his term of office. They were right. In less than a year after Ford took office, President Nixon resigned rather than face an impeachment trial on three charges of misconduct in office. Gerald R. Ford became president on August

9, 1974, and served out the last two years of Richard Nixon's term.

President Ford is credited with leading the country during the difficult, chaotic days after the Watergate crisis, when the confidence of the people in the presidency had been severely shattered. He has also been criticized for pardoning Richard Nixon before he could be brought to trial. At the Republican convention in 1976, Ford was renominated as the party's presidential candidate, and he chose Senator Robert Dole of Kansas as his running mate. They were defeated by Jimmy Carter and Senator Walter Mondale in the fall elections.

After his defeat, Ford retired to California, where he continued to take part in politics as a Republican leader and spokesman.

3

Who Ever Heard
of Hannibal Hamlin?

From 1805, when George Clinton was elected as Thomas Jefferson's vice-president, until 1945, when Vice-President Harry S. Truman was suddenly thrust into the presidency during a time of war, the vice-presidents of the United States were obscure men, often not too well known even when they ran for office. And they were usually soon forgotten by history. As Harry Truman said to Robert Hannegan, chairman of the Democratic National Committee, who was trying to persuade him to accept the vice-presidential nomination: "Bob, I bet I can go down on the street and stop the first ten men I see and they can't tell me the names of the last ten vice-presidents."

It was during the years of the nineteenth and early twentieth centuries that the office became famous for its unimportance, years that inspired the story Thomas Riley Marshall, who was vice-president under Woodrow Wilson, used to tell: "Once there were two brothers. One ran away to sea; the other was elected vice-president of the United States. And nothing was heard of either of them again."

Most of the vice-presidents discussed in this chapter are like Vice-President Marshall himself—virtually unknown in American history, despite the fact that they held the second highest office in the government. Some, like Aaron Burr, are famous for reasons other than the

Hubert H. Humphrey, Democratic candidate for president in 1968, for whom Democrats here are demonstrating at the 1968 convention, was vice-president from 1965 to 1969. Humphrey said of the office: "There is a special kind of excitement, tension, and drama in being so close to executive power. You cannot escape the recurring thought that you could be president someday."

Hubert H. Humphrey was also one of the nation's great orators, the leading liberal voice of his era, and among the most capable legislators ever to sit in the Senate. The Department of Health, Education and Welfare building in Washington is named after him. He died in 1978 and is remembered as one of his country's and party's most beloved statesmen.

fact that they served in the vice-presidency. And a few are well known today, like Hubert H. Humphrey, who was a great senator and a presidential candidate. But he too may fade into history unremembered, unknown.

50

Aaron Burr, 1801–1805

Even though he never went on to become president, Aaron Burr achieved fame in his own right. For one thing, while he was still vice-president, he fought a duel in which he killed Alexander Hamilton, one of the most brilliant of our country's early statesmen. And after he had been indicted for murder (because dueling was illegal in New York where the duel took place), Burr, still vice-president, presided over the Senate and the impeachment of Associate Supreme Court Justice Samuel Chase. Chase was found innocent and Burr conducted the impeachment trial with such fairness that even his worst enemies praised his performance.

Burr was born in Newark, New Jersey, in 1756. His father was president of what is now Princeton University. He entered the College of New Jersey, as Princeton was then called, at the age of thirteen and graduated in three years with honors, in 1772. After studying theology for a brief period, he took up law, but interrupted his studies to fight in the Revolution.

Burr was a valiant soldier. But after four years in the army he

retired because of ill health and resumed the study of law. He was admitted to the bar in 1782, practiced law briefly in Albany, then moved to New York City and went into politics, serving in the New York assembly from 1784 to 1785. In 1789 he was appointed attorney general and served in that post until 1791, when he was elected for one term to the U.S. Senate. He returned to New York in 1797 to run for the assembly again, won, served one term, and then was defeated.

His next move was to begin a reorganization of the Democratic-Republican party in New York for the presidential election of 1800. This led to his being picked as Thomas Jefferson's running mate. At that time, the president and vice-president were voted for separately and Burr and Jefferson appeared to have won the election, but confusion in the electoral college produced a tie. Both Jefferson and Burr were given an equal number of votes and Burr declined to accept the vice-presidency. Under the Constitution, a tie had to be settled in the House of Representatives with each of the then sixteen states having one vote. On the thirty-sixth ballot, Jefferson was elected president and Burr acceded to the vice-presidency.

Burr presided with distinction over the Senate, but he felt sure Jefferson would drop him from the ticket in 1804. So he decided to run for the governorship of New York. He lost the election—in part because he was opposed by Alexander Hamilton with whom he had long been feuding. Learning of some slanderous remark Hamilton made about him, Burr challenged him to a duel and killed him. Although he served out his term as vice-president, the duel with Hamilton ended his political career.

Burr left Washington and went to New Orleans where he became involved in a plan to establish a new republic. He was tried for treason but was found not guilty. From 1808 to 1812, he lived in Europe in poverty. Then he returned to America to practice law. He died in 1836 at the age of eighty on Staten Island, New York.

George Clinton, 1805–1812

George Clinton was the first, and one of the few vice-presidents, to serve under two different presidents.

Clinton was born in Little Britain, New York, in 1739. When he was eighteen, he left home to become a sailor but returned to fight in the French and Indian War. After the war, he studied law and was admitted to the bar in Ulster County, New York. He was elected to the provincial assembly in 1768, where he quickly became a leader of the anti-British group. In 1775, he was elected one of New York's delegates to the Second Continental Congress, but he did not sign the Declaration of Independence because he was serving with the Continental Army at the time, as a brigadier general.

Clinton helped draft New York State's constitution and was elected the state's first governor, which helped earn him the title "father" of New York. He served six successive terms, from 1777 to 1795. At the Constitutional Convention of 1787, he opposed the Constitution because he felt it gave the federal government too much power over the states. He set forth his views in a series of articles, which he signed with the name "Cato," in the New York *Journal.* Alexander Hamilton, using the name "Caesar," took issue with them in the New York *Daily Advertiser.*

In 1804, Clinton was nominated to run as Jefferson's vice-presidential candidate. After they were elected, he felt he should be the party's next presidential candidate. But the nomination went instead to James Madison, and Clinton was elected vice-president again. He died in office—the first vice-president to do so—in 1812, at the age of seventy-two.

Elbridge Gerry, 1813–1814

Elbridge Gerry, who was one of two vice-presidents who died in office, is the only one buried in Washington, D.C.

Gerry was born in Marblehead, Massachusetts, in 1744. His father was a wealthy merchant, and after he graduated from Harvard in 1762, he worked in his father's shipping business. In 1772, he was elected to the Massachusetts legislature, and from 1776 to 1781 he was a delegate to the Second Continental Congress. He favored separation from Great Britain and fully supported the Declaration of Independence, which he signed. He was also a delegate to the Constitutional Convention and, although he opposed the Constitution, he supported it once it was agreed upon.

From 1789 to 1793, Gerry served in Congress, then retired from politics to take care of his business interest. In 1797, he was appointed a member of a three-man commission to negotiate a commercial treaty with France. He was criticized for staying on after the other members of the commission—John Marshall and Charles C. Pinckney—had returned home.

In 1800, Gerry began running for the governorship of Massachusetts and was defeated four straight times before he finally won in 1810. He was re-elected in 1811, and, during his second term, Gerry signed a bill that gave him more historical prominence than any other thing he ever did. The bill reshaped the state's election districts in such a way as to put most of them under control of his party. One new district was thought to resemble a salamander and critics of the scheme thought it ought to be called a "Gerrymander." To this day, any effort to reshape an election district so that it favors one party is known as a gerrymander.

In 1812, the Democratic-Republican party nominated Gerry to run as vice-president with James Madison after Gerry was defeated for re-election in Massachusetts. They won and Gerry took office in 1813. But the following year, at the age of seventy, he died suddenly while on his way to the Senate.

Daniel D. Tompkins, 1817–1825

Daniel D. Tompkins served eight years as vice-president and yet is virtually unknown today. He was born in what is now Scarsdale, New York, in 1774. After he graduated from Columbia College in 1795, he studied law, and in 1797 was admitted to the bar. In 1801, he served as a member of a New York State convention, which revised the state constitution. Then, like most lawyers of this period, he was drawn into politics. In 1803, he was elected to the New York legislature and the next year to the U.S. House of Representatives. However, he resigned before the term began to accept an appointment to the New York Supreme Court.

In 1807, he ran for the governorship of New York. He won and was re-elected three times. As governor, he urged the legislature to pass legislation outlawing slavery in New York, and he achieved a reputation as a liberal governor. During the War of 1812, he contributed a substantial amount of his own fortune in the fight against Great Britain. However, his career was plagued by constant rumors that he had cheated New York State out of the money. Not until 1824 did Congress establish the fact that Tompkins was innocent and the government, in fact, owed him $94,000.

In 1816, he was re-elected governor of New York and at the same time was elected vice-president of the United States (which was possible under New York law) under President James Monroe on the Democratic-Republican ticket. Tompkins ran for governor of New York again in 1820, but was defeated by De Witt Clinton. However, he was elected for a second term as Monroe's vice-president. He died three months after his second term at the relatively young age of fifty-one. The long fight to preserve his reputation and regain his fortune had taken its toll.

John C. Calhoun, 1825–1832

John C. Calhoun served nearly two full terms as vice-president under two different presidents and, until Spiro T. Agnew's resignation in 1974, was the only vice-president to resign from the office. However, he is primarily known in history as a great southern senator and advocate of states' rights.

Calhoun was born on a farm near Abbeville, South Carolina, in 1782. He had little formal education in rural schools, but enough to gain admittance to Yale, from which he graduated in 1804. In 1807, he opened a law practice in Abbeville and went almost immediately into politics. In 1808 and 1809, he was elected to the South Carolina legislature, and in 1810 he was elected to the House of Representatives. He quickly gained a reputation as a great orator and joined with the "War Hawks" who were in favor of war with Great Britain. When war came, he worked tirelessly in the Congress to pass legislation supporting the war effort.

Calhoun remained in Congress until 1817, when he resigned to become secretary of war in President James Monroe's administration. He served two full terms in that post; then, in 1824, he was elected vice-president with President John Quincy Adams. Calhoun was considered a leading candidate for the Democratic presidential nomination four years later, but he had to step aside because of the popularity of Andrew Jackson. He became Jackson's vice-presidential running mate, and when they were elected, Calhoun was considered the heir apparent to the presidency.

By 1832, however, Calhoun and Jackson had developed serious philosophical, political, and personal differences. Just before his vice-presidential term was up, Calhoun ran for and won a seat in the Senate. He resigned from the vice-presidency, and was not replaced because there was no provision in the Constitution then for the replacement of a vice-president.

Except for a brief period in 1844–45, when he served as President Tyler's secretary of state, Calhoun remained in the Senate until his death at the age of sixty-eight, in 1850. His last years in the Senate were marked by strong support of slavery in the South and the annexation of Texas.

Richard M. Johnson, 1837–1841

Richard M. Johnson was born in 1780 on the Kentucky frontier. His schooling was spotty until he began to study law at Transylvania University. He was admitted to the bar in 1802 and became active in state politics as a "Jeffersonian Republican." He was elected to the Kentucky legislature in 1804 and served there until he entered the U.S. House of Representatives in 1807. While still a congressman, he fought in the War of 1812, serving under General William Henry Harrison as a Kentucky rifleman. He was wounded in the battle of the Thames in 1813 and gained fame as the man thought to have killed the Indian leader Tecumseh.

After the war, Johnson became a Democrat, returning to the House until 1819, when he retired. Then he was elected again to the Kentucky legislature, which appointed him to the U.S. Senate, where he served until 1829. He was a loyal supporter of the leading Democrat of his day, Andrew Jackson, who hand picked Johnson to serve as Martin Van Buren's running mate in 1836. Although Van Buren received a majority of votes for president, none of the four candidates for vice-president received a majority in the electoral college. So under the Constitution, the Senate decided by voting on the two leading candidates. Johnson won.

Johnson's vice-presidency was undistinguished and he gradually became alienated from his party. He was not renominated to run with Van Buren in 1840, and he returned to Kentucky where he served for a time in the Kentucky legislature. He died in 1850.

George M. Dallas, 1845–1849

George M. Dallas was born in 1792 in Philadelphia, Pennsylvania. His father, Alexander Dallas, was a lawyer who would later become James Madison's secretary of the treasury. After young Dallas graduated from the College of New Jersey (now Princeton) in 1810, he studied law with his father. He was admitted to the bar in 1813, the same year his father arranged for him to serve as private secretary to Albert Gallatin, United States minister to Russia. In this capacity, young Dallas took part in the peace negotiations with England after the War of 1812, and in 1814 he returned to the United States from London with the first British peace offer.

After the war, Dallas worked briefly for his father, who was serving as secretary of the treasury. Then he returned to Philadelphia to practice law and serve on the legal staff of the Second Bank of the United States. He was also an active Democrat, and in 1831 he was appointed to fill an unexpired term in the Senate. In 1833, he began a two-year term as Pennsylvania's attorney general. In 1837, President Martin Van Buren appointed him U.S. minister to Russia.

In 1839, he returned to Philadelphia to practice law, but he continued his active interest in politics. In 1844, he was nominated vice-presidential candidate to run with James K. Polk, and they defeated the Whig candidate, Henry Clay. As vice-president, Dallas cast the tie-breaking vote in the Senate that resulted in the passage of the historic Tariff Act of 1846.

When Polk announced that he would not be a candidate for a second term, Dallas was passed over at the Democratic convention. After the election Dallas returned to Philadelphia to practice law. Then he was appointed minister to Great Britain from 1856 to 1861. He died in Philadelphia in 1864 at the age of seventy-two.

William R. King, 1853

William R. King is the only vice-president to take the oath of office on foreign soil, but he died before he ever served.

King was born in Sampson County, North Carolina, in 1786. After graduating from the University of North Carolina in 1803, he studied law and was admitted to the bar in 1806. And, like most future office holders, he went immediately into politics, serving in the North Carolina legislature through 1809. In 1810, he was elected to the U.S. House of Representatives. He was twenty-four when elected, but turned twenty-five by the time he took office, just barely old enough to qualify. In 1816, he was appointed secretary of the U.S. legation in Russia. He returned to settle in Alabama in 1818, and the following year when Alabama was admitted to the Union, King was elected one of the new state's first senators.

King served in the Senate until 1844—five years as president pro tempore—and gradually became known for his capabilities. In 1844, President Tyler appointed him minister to France, where his primary mission was to persuade France not to join Britain in objecting to the annexation of Texas. He was successful; but he was less successful when he returned to Alabama in 1846 to seek re-election to the Senate. Two years later, he was appointed to a vacant seat in the Senate and was later re-elected to a full term.

King served in the Senate until 1852, when he was nominated vice-presidential candidate by the Democrats. He had supported James Buchanan for president, but when Franklin Pierce was nominated instead, King was offered the vice-presidency to placate Buchanan's followers.

Pierce and King were elected, but King was in the final stages of tuberculosis. After the election, he went to Cuba seeking a cure, but was unsuccessful. By inauguration day, he felt too weak to return to the United States to take the oath of office, so Congress passed a special act enabling him to take the oath in Cuba. He left Cuba in April of 1853 and returned to his home in Alabama, where he died, leaving the office of vice-president empty for the four years of Franklin Pierce's term.

John C. Breckinridge, 1857–1861

John C. Breckinridge, the youngest man ever to be sworn in as vice-president, was born near Lexington, Kentucky, in 1821. He graduated from Centre College in Kentucky in 1838 (and also attended what is now Princeton) before taking up the study of law in Kentucky, where he was admitted to the bar. He practiced law in several states before settling down in Lexington. In 1847, he was commissioned a major in a Kentucky volunteer regiment and served briefly in the Mexican War. Two years later, he was elected to the Kentucky state legislature, and in 1851 he was elected to the U.S. House of Representatives. By 1855, he had achieved a national reputation as an orator and statesman and was leader of the Kentucky Democratic party. However, he declined a diplomatic post abroad and refused a third term in the House in order to return to Kentucky to practice law. The following year, the Democratic convention elected him as James Buchanan's running mate, hoping that his popularity would help him carry Kentucky and other southern states.

Buchanan and Breckinridge won and the Kentucky lawyer was sworn in as vice-president at the age of thirty-six. The young vice-president distinguished himself, despite the fact that he was pro-slavery, as he presided over the Senate in the difficult days leading up to the Civil War. He was so popular in his home state that in a special election in 1859 Kentucky elected him to fill a Senate seat two years hence, when his term as vice-president would presumably be ended. In 1860, the southern wing of the Democratic party, known as the Independent Democratic party, nominated him for president, but he lost to Abraham Lincoln. In his last few months in the vice-presidency, he continued to preside over the Senate, trying to work out a solution to the slavery issue. After he took his seat in the Senate, Breckinridge became an outspoken critic of Lincoln's war measures. When war broke out in 1861, Kentucky chose to remain neutral. But Breckinridge clearly sided with the Confederacy, and after he introduced various proposals obviously designed to aid the South, a federal grand jury indicted him for treason. The Senate banished him as a traitor and Breckinridge sought refuge in the Confederate states. He fought in the Confederate Army as a brigadier general, seeing action in the battles of Shiloh, Vicksburg, Murfreesboro, and Chickamauga. In the Shenandoah campaign, he was Jeb Stuart's second-in-command. In February of 1865, he was made secretary of war in the Confederacy.

After the war, Breckinridge fled to Europe where he remained until the amnesty proclamation of 1868 made it possible for him to return to Kentucky and his law practice. He died in 1875.

Hannibal Hamlin, 1861–1865

Hannibal Hamlin is one of the least remembered vice-presidents of the United States even though he served under one of the most famous presidents in history—Abraham Lincoln.

Hamlin was born in Paris Hill, Maine, in 1809. He graduated from

Hebron Academy but had to abandon his plans for a college education when his father died. He worked on his mother's farm, was a schoolteacher, surveyor, and co-publisher of a small newspaper before he finally began to study law in Portland. In 1833, he was admitted to the bar and began to practice law in Hampden, Maine. He soon became active in politics, serving in the Maine legislature from 1836 to 1841. In 1842, he was elected to the U.S. House of Representatives. In 1846, he was defeated in an effort to win a seat in the Senate, but later in a special election was voted to complete an unexpired term. In 1850, he was re-elected for a full term.

Hamlin was outspoken against slavery, which eventually led to his break with the Democratic party and his shift to the Republican party. In 1856, he was elected the first Republican governor of Maine. However, he only served a few weeks in the job before he resigned to run for the Senate in a special election. As a former Democrat and an easterner, he was a logical choice to run with Abraham Lincoln in 1860. They won, and as vice-president, Hamlin remained devoted to Lincoln, although he was sympathetic to the more conservative radical wing of the party. Hamlin was with Lincoln at Gettysburg when the president delivered his famous address.

In 1864, the Republicans decided a southern Democrat who had remained loyal to the Union would help the ticket, so they chose Andrew Johnson over Hamlin. When Lincoln was assassinated in 1865, President Johnson appointed Hamlin collector of the port of Boston. However, he resigned that post the following year in protest against Johnson's reconstruction policies. In 1868, he was re-elected to the Senate and returned to Washington to join the Republican radicals in their opposition to President Johnson. Hamlin served in the Senate until 1881, when President James Garfield appointed him minister to Spain. He returned to the United States in 1883 and retired to Bangor, Maine, where he remained active in Republican politics until his death in 1891.

Schuyler Colfax, 1869–1873

Schuyler Colfax was born in New York City in 1823, but his family moved to Indiana when he was thirteen. He worked as a store clerk and as assistant to his father, who was auditor of St. Joseph County. He was interested in politics, and for a short time served as a clerk in the state senate, then as a correspondent for the *Indiana State Journal.* He also studied law, but was never admitted to the bar. In 1845, he bought an interest in the *South Bend Free Press,* changed its name to *St. Joseph Valley Register,* and became a successful newspaper editor for eighteen years. He was also active in politics, becoming a Republican in 1854, when he was elected to the U.S. House of Representatives. Eventually he became Speaker of the House, and, by 1868, was a leading member of the radical wing of the Republican party. He was considered for the Republican presidential nomination in 1868. But the nomination went to the Civil War hero Ulysses S. Grant, and Colfax was picked as his vice-presidential running mate. The Republicans won.

Although Grant and Colfax were nearly the same age and similar in appearance, they differed in temperament. When Grant became convinced that Colfax was scheming to become president in 1872, he let it be known that he intended to dump Colfax from the ticket. Colfax was ruined politically when it was discovered near the end of his vice-presidency that earlier he had been involved in the Credit Mobilier railroad scandals, in which a number of corrupt politicians and businessmen had plotted to cheat the government out of millions of dollars. There was talk of impeaching Colfax, but the scandal broke so near the end of his term that nothing was done.

After he left the vice-presidency, Colfax traveled the country on lecture tours and eventually died in Mankato, Minnesota, in 1885.

Henry Wilson, 1873–1875

Henry Wilson was born in Farmington, New Hampshire, in 1812. His original name was Jeremiah Jones Colbath, but he changed his name when he reached the age of twenty-one. His father was a laborer in a saw mill and Wilson grew up in poverty with little formal schooling. From 1822 to 1823, he worked on farms, then moved to Natick,

Massachusetts, where he worked as a shoemaker for several years, acquiring the nickname "The Natick Cobbler." He built a successful shoe business, at one time employing over 100 people. Visiting the state of Virginia for his health, and later listening to the slavery debates in Congress, Wilson became a foe of slavery and decided to enter politics as a dedicated abolitionist. In 1840, he was elected to the Massachusetts legislature and was re-elected several times. He became known throughout Massachusetts for his antislavery speeches. In 1848, he helped found the Free-Soil party when the Whig convention failed to endorse the Wilmot Proviso, which prohibited slavery in the territory acquired from Mexico. In the early 1850s, while serving in the state senate, he joined the Know-Nothing party, but withdrew because he disapproved of its stand on slavery. In 1855, a coalition of antislavery Democrats, Free-Soilers, and Know-Nothings elected him to fill a vacancy in the U.S. Senate. He was re-elected the following year and remained in the Senate until 1873. He was one of the founders of the Republican party and during the war he served as chairman of the Senate committee on military affairs, where he showed exceptional ability in helping prepare the nation for war.

Following the war, he was one of the radical Republicans who advocated strict reconstruction policies for the South. He was a candidate for the vice-presidency in 1868, but was passed over for Schuyler Colfax. In 1872, after Colfax had been dropped from the office by President Grant, Wilson was nominated to run as Grant's vice-presidential candidate. They won, and as Wilson was entering the vice-presidency, it was learned that, like Colfax, he had also bought shares in the corrupt Credit Mobilier Corporation. But Wilson had returned the shares and he survived the scandal. During his vice-presidency, Wilson spent considerable time writing a three-volume work entitled *History of the Rise and Fall of Slave Power in America*. In 1875, while still vice-president, he suffered a paralytic stroke in the Capitol and died within two weeks.

William A. Wheeler, 1877–1881

William A. Wheeler was born in Malone, New York, in 1819. Wheeler's father died when he was young and he had to work his way through school. He attended the University of Vermont for two years before financial difficulties forced him to leave. He began the study of law and in 1845 was admitted to the bar in New York. The following year, he was elected Franklin County district attorney. In 1849, he was elected to the New York state legislature and in 1858 to the New York senate.

In 1860, Wheeler was elected to one term in the U.S. House of Representatives, and in 1867–68 he presided over the New York state constitutional convention. In the Republican landslide of 1868 he was re-elected to the House, where he served until 1877. In the House, he was known as a man of utmost integrity at a time when many politicians were thought to be dishonest. He opposed the famous "Salary Grab" of 1873 that increased the salaries of many government officials. When it was passed, he refused to accept the salary increase.

In 1876, the Republican convention picked Rutherford B. Hayes of Ohio as its presidential candidate and, to balance the ticket geographically, chose Wheeler as the vice-presidential nominee. The Republicans defeated Democrats Samuel Tilden and Thomas Hendricks in a close election, which was eventually decided by a commission created by a special act of Congress. Wheeler was a good presiding officer in the Senate and a close and loyal friend of President Hayes, who said Wheeler's character was "sterling gold." However, their administration was undistinguished and neither Wheeler nor Hayes was considered by the party for renomination in 1880. Wheeler retired to upstate New York where he died in 1887 at the age of sixty-seven.

Thomas A. Hendricks, 1885

From 1868 to 1884, Thomas A. Hendricks was a candidate for president in every election but one. When he was finally elected vice-president he died eight months after taking office.

Hendricks was born near Zanesville, Ohio, in 1819. His family moved to a farm in Indiana when he was young, and he received his early education in Indiana academies before attending Hanover College. When he graduated in 1841, he studied law in Indiana and Pennsylvania before being admitted to the bar in 1843. He began his law practice in Shelbyville, Indiana, and in 1848 he was elected to the Indiana legislature. In 1850, he played a prominent part in the Indiana constitutional convention. He was also elected to the U.S. House of Representatives that year, where he remained until 1855. President Franklin Pierce appointed him head of the General Land Office, where he made a national reputation as an honest and efficient administrator. He resigned in 1859 because of differences with President James Buchanan and went back to practice law in Indianapolis. In the following year, he was defeated in an effort to win the governorship of Indiana; but in 1863, in a wave of popular reaction against the Civil War, he was elected to the U.S. Senate. In the Senate, Hendricks opposed the draft, emancipation, the issuance of greenbacks, and the radical reconstruction policies. He voted against the impeachment of Andrew Johnson. And in 1868, while still a senator, he was again an unsuccessful candidate for the governor of Indiana, as well as for his party's presidential nomination.

He left the Senate in 1869 and returned to Indianapolis to practice law. In 1872, he was elected governor of Indiana. Four years later, he was nominated vice-presidential candidate with Samuel J. Tilden, and although they beat Hayes and Wheeler in the popular vote, they lost the disputed election, which was eventually settled by a congressional committee. Hendricks continued to practice law and in 1884 he was nominated as vice-presidential candidate with Grover Cleveland. In one of the most bitter and unsavory campaigns in American history, Cleveland and Hendricks beat the Republicans under James G. Blaine. But Hendricks died suddenly of a stroke eight months after taking office. He was sixty-five.

Levi P. Morton, 1889–1893

Levi P. Morton was so fair in presiding over the Senate that it
may have cost him the vice-presidential renomination. Morton was
born in Shoreham, Vermont, in 1824. He received a scanty education
and at fourteen began working in a store. By the time he was nineteen,
he had his own mercantile business in Hanover, New Hampshire.

Six years later, he went to work for a Boston company and was soon made a junior partner. J. Spencer Morgan, the father of J. Pierpont Morgan, was a senior partner. Just before the Civil War, Morton established his own dry goods business in New York, but it went bankrupt because of the Civil War. After the war, he organized L. P. Morton and Company, which emerged as one of the most prominent Wall Street banking firms in the country. As his banking business prospered, Morton decided to enter politics, running for Congress as a Republican from New York City at the age of fifty-three. He was defeated. However, two years later, in 1878, he was elected. Then he gave up his seat to serve as U.S. minister to France from 1881 to 1885.

After being defeated for a seat in the Senate in 1886, he bought a dairy farm in upstate New York. He ran for the Senate again in 1887, but was unsuccessful. In 1888, the Republicans nominated him vice-presidential candidate to run with Benjamin Harrison. They were elected.

Morton was one of the fairest vice-presidents ever to preside over the Senate. Republicans controlled the Senate but he refused to join forces with his party members in efforts to block the Democratic minority with procedural tactics. In one heated debate, Morton refused to go out to lunch rather than permit Republicans to take advantage of his absence. As a result, Morton was looked upon with disfavor by his party and it probably contributed to his not being renominated for the vice-presidency, although Harrison was renominated in the 1892 election. The Republicans chose instead Whitelaw Reid, editor of the *New York Herald Tribune,* but they were defeated by the Democrats. Members of the Senate in both parties paid unusual tribute to Morton by giving him a banquet when he left office.

Two years later, Morton was elected governor of New York and served in that office until 1897. Then he retired to his country estate, where he lived until 1920. He was ninety-six when he died.

Adlai E. Stevenson, 1893–1897

Adlai E. Stevenson was the grandfather of Adlai Stevenson, the Democratic candidate for president in 1952 and 1956. The elder Stevenson was born in Christian County, Kentucky, in 1835. His father was a farmer and slaveholder. When he was sixteen, his family moved to Bloomington, Illinois. He attended Illinois Wesleyan University and Centre College in Kentucky. He left college before graduation because of the death of his father and took up the study of law privately. He was admitted to the bar in 1857, and the following year he opened a law office in Metamora, Illinois. Ten years later, he began practicing law in Bloomington.

Stevenson was an active Democrat and for a time served as state attorney. In 1874, he ran for Congress in a heavily Republican district and won. He was defeated in 1876, but was re-elected in 1878. He was defeated in 1880. Five years later, President Grover Cleveland appointed him assistant postmaster general. In 1892, when Grover Cleveland was nominated by the Democrats for a second term, he picked Stevenson as his running mate. Cleveland's first vice-president, Thomas Hendricks, had died in office. They were elected, and during his term in office, Stevenson differed with President Cleveland on economic matters. He and a number of friends and advisers who also differed with Cleveland became known as the "Stevenson cabinet" and were vocal on their opposition to Cleveland's views on money and the gold standard. In 1896, when the Democrats nominated William Jennings Bryan as their presidential candidate, Stevenson was not renominated. Instead, the Democrats nominated Arthur Sewall of Maine. Bryan and Sewall were defeated, and four years later, when the Democrats renominated Bryan, they renominated Stevenson as his vice-presidential running mate. They were also defeated. Like his grandson, Stevenson was a witty man and often joked about the anonymous role of the vice-president in American government. He advised his grandson never to seek the office.

After he retired from the vice-presidency, Stevenson was defeated in an effort to win the governorship of Illinois in 1908. He retired from politics and wrote a book, *Something of Men I Have Known*. He died in 1914.

Garret A. Hobart, 1897–1899

Although Garret A. Hobart was considered one of the most capable and effective vice-presidents in our history, his primary claim to fame might well be that his death opened the door to the vice-presidency, and then the presidency, of one of America's most forceful and important presidents—Theodore Roosevelt.

Hobart was born in Long Branch, New Jersey, in 1844. He graduated from Rutgers College in 1863 and, after a brief period of teaching, began to study law in Paterson, New Jersey. He was admitted to the bar in 1866. Hobart also became active in politics and quickly emerged as one of the leaders in the New Jersey Republican party. In 1871, he was chosen counsel for the city of Paterson and the following year was elected to the state assembly. In 1876, he was elected to the state senate, where he served until 1882. He was also elected speaker of the senate, was chairman of the state Republican committee and a member of the Republican National Committee.

Although Hobart never served in a major political office (he was defeated in a try for a U.S. Senate seat in 1884), he was a powerful figure in Republican politics. As a popular Republican in a large, normally Democratic state, he was a logical choice as a vice-presidential candidate. At their convention in 1896, the Republicans nominated William McKinley and Hobart, and they defeated Democrats Bryan and Sewall in the fall elections.

Hobart served only half of his term but, before he died he worked out a good relationship with President McKinley and is considered by many historians to have revived the prestige of the office simply by his conduct and approach to the vice-presidency.

Charles W. Fairbanks, 1905–1909

Charles W. Fairbanks was born in a log cabin near Unionville Center, Ohio, in 1852. He grew up on a farm and worked his way through Ohio Wesleyan University. After graduation, he worked for the Associated Press in Pittsburgh and Cleveland in the daytime and studied law at night. He was admitted to the bar in 1874 and then set up his law practice in Indianapolis. He became an extremely successful lawyer, specializing in railroad cases. At the same time, he gained recognition as an Indiana Republican leader. In 1893, he ran for a Senate seat in a special election and was defeated. In 1896, he was picked as temporary chairman and keynote speaker at the Republican National Convention that nominated William McKinley. In another special election, in 1897, he was elected to the Senate, where he was a strong supporter of President McKinley. He became a prominent member of several important Senate committees and an unofficial spokesman for the McKinley administration. In 1898, he was appointed a member of the commission charged with settling a U.S.-Canadian boundary dispute, and in 1902 he was re-elected to the Senate.

President McKinley was assassinated in 1901, making Vice-President Theodore Roosevelt president. At the Republican convention in 1904, Roosevelt was renominated for the presidency and, to balance the ticket with a conservative Republican close to McKinley, the convention chose Fairbanks. Roosevelt and Fairbanks were elected in a landslide over the Democrats, Alton B. Parker and Henry G. Davis.

In his second term, Roosevelt continued to feud with his Republican colleagues in the Senate and Fairbanks sided with Roosevelt's enemies. The bitterness between Roosevelt and Fairbanks was at times so great that once when Roosevelt was considering taking a submarine trip, American humorist Finley Peter Dunne said Roosevelt should not do so "unless you take Fairbanks with you." Roosevelt decided not to run again in 1908, but he hand picked his successor, William Howard Taft.

Annoyed at having the liberal Roosevelt dictate his successor, the convention passed over Fairbanks to pick an ultra-conservative running mate for Taft, James S. Sherman.

After leaving office, Fairbanks returned to private life but remained active in politics. He was Indiana's "favorite son" candidate in 1916, but he accepted the vice-presidential nomination with Charles Evans Hughes. They were defeated. Two years later, Fairbanks died in Indianapolis at the age of sixty-six.

James S. Sherman, 1909–1912

James S. Sherman is the only vice-presidential candidate in history to receive three million votes after he was dead.

Sherman was born in Utica, New York, in 1855. He attended Hamilton College, from which he graduated in 1878 and received a law degree in 1879. He became a prominent lawyer and was active in Republican politics. In 1884, he was elected mayor of Utica, and two years later he was elected to the U.S. House of Representatives. From 1887 until 1909, he missed only one term in the House. His record there was undistinguished, but he was known as a good party man. At the Republican convention in 1909, President Theodore Roosevelt picked William Howard Taft as his successor. The Republicans did not trust Roosevelt or Taft, whom they considered liberals, and chose Sherman as Taft's running mate, insisting on balancing the ticket with a good Republican conservative.

Taft and Sherman were elected but soon had a falling out. Taft wanted Sherman to be his liaison with the House of Representatives because Taft did not like House Speaker Joe Cannon. Sherman, who liked Cannon, refused, saying: "I am vice-president, and acting as a messenger boy is not part of my duties. . . ." The president and vice-president also had another serious dispute over control of the Republican party in New York State.

Despite their disagreements, the Republicans renominated them at the 1912 convention. Sherman died six days before the election, but more than three million people voted for him anyway. The electoral college gave his votes to Nicholas Murray Butler, president of Columbia University. Butler consented, only, as he put it, "as long as there is no chance of my being elected vice-president." Butler's wish obviously was granted, as the election was won by the Democratic candidates Woodrow Wilson and Thomas R. Marshall.

Thomas R. Marshall, 1913–1921

Thomas R. Marshall was one of the country's most popular vice-presidents. During his last few days in office, he was faced with a crisis that dramatized the need for clearly defining the constitutional role of the vice-president.

Marshall was born in North Manchester, Indiana, in 1854. After many moves and many schools, the Marshall family resettled in Indiana. Marshall graduated from Wabash College in 1873. He studied law in a Fort Wayne law office and was admitted to the bar in 1875. He practiced law in Columbia City, Indiana, where he developed an interest in Democratic politics. In 1908, he was elected governor of Indiana. He served one term in which he managed to put through a number of reforms, including a child labor law. In 1912, he was entered as a "favorite son" candidate for president, but the nomination went to Woodrow Wilson. Wilson chose Marshall as his running mate, and they handily beat the badly split Republican party candidates.

Marshall was an excellent vice-president, loyal to President Wilson and well known for his wit. Once, after presiding over a Senate debate concerning the needs of the country, he remarked: "What this country needs is a good five-cent cigar." His remark became part of our humorous literature.

Wilson and Marshall were re-elected in 1916. After World War I, when President Wilson went to Europe to attend the peace conferences, he requested that Marshall preside over meetings of the cabinet in his absence. And in Wilson's last months in office, when he suffered a stroke and was incapacitated, many people urged Marshall to step in and assume the powers of the presidency. Marshall said no, he would be accused of seizing power unconstitutionally and that it might even lead to civil war. The situation convinced most students of government that a constitutional amendment was needed to deal with the question of what happens when a president is incapacitated.

In 1921, Marshall returned to his law practice in Indiana and wrote a book that became very popular, *Recollections of Thomas R. Marshall.* He died in 1925, the same year the book was published, at the age of seventy-one.

Charles G. Dawes, 1925–1929

Charles G. Dawes was born in Marietta, Ohio, in 1865. He graduated from Marietta College in 1884 and studied law at the University of Cincinnati. In 1887, he began to practice law in Lincoln, Nebraska. Seven years later, his interest in public utilities law took him to Chicago and he settled in Evanston, Illinois. He was a Republican and in 1896 he campaigned for William McKinley, which led to a warm friendship with the presidential candidate. When McKinley was elected, he appointed Dawes comptroller of currency. He held the office from 1898 until 1902, returning to private life to organize and become president of the Central Trust Company of Illinois. He served as a brigadier general in World War I and remained in the army after the war to dispose of some $400 million in surplus equipment. In 1921, President Harding appointed Dawes the first director of the budget, and, in 1923, he was appointed head of a group of international financial experts charged with solving economic problems growing out of the German reparations—that is, money Germany owed after its defeat in 1918. The group developed what came to be known as the "Dawes Plan," which saved the economy of Europe and resulted in the Nobel Peace Prize being awarded jointly to Dawes and the British foreign secretary, Sir Austen Chamberlain.

The acclaim given the Dawes Plan made Dawes a national figure, and at the 1924 Republican National Convention, when their first choice for the vice-presidential candidate refused to accept the nomination, Dawes was selected. The convention had preferred Governor Frank Lowden of Illinois, but he refused to run with Calvin Coolidge because he disapproved of the Coolidge agriculture program. This made Lowden only the second man in history to decline the office.

Coolidge and Dawes were elected, but Dawes had a difficult time as vice-president. He alienated the president by sending him a letter saying he did not want to serve in the cabinet because it would be a bad precedent. This was presumptuous, especially since the vice-president did not, as a rule, serve in the cabinet and Coolidge had not indicated that he planned to ask Dawes to do so. He also alienated the Senate almost as soon as he took office by lecturing it on the evils of the filibuster. The Senate felt Dawes had shown poor judgment and worse taste. Finally, he became something of a national joke when he took a nap on the day a very important vote in the Senate came close enough to necessitate the vice-president's vote to break a tie. The vote concerned Coolidge's appointment of Charles Warren for attorney general. The vote did come to a tie, but before Dawes could be summoned from his nap and transported in a wild taxi ride to the Senate, a Democratic senator reversed his vote and defeated Warren. Coolidge and the Republicans were furious at Dawes. His vice-presidency was a disappointment, too, in that he failed in efforts to streamline the rules of the Senate.

Dawes continued an active career after he retired from the vice-presidency, serving as ambassador to Great Britain and chairman of the Reconstruction Finance Corporation. He was also active in the banking business and wrote several books on banking before he died in 1951 at the age of eighty-five.

Charles Curtis, 1929–1933

Charles Curtis was the only vice-president of part Indian descent. He was born in 1860 on a farm on Indian land in Kansas. When his mother died, he went to live on an Indian reservation with his grandmother, who was the daughter of a Kaw chief. In 1879, after three years of high school, he began the study of law and was admitted to the bar two years later. He also became active in Republican politics and served as attorney for Shawnee County in Kansas before being elected to the U.S. House of Representatives in 1892. He won a Senate seat in 1906, was defeated in 1912, but was re-elected in 1914 and served in the Senate for the next fourteen years. Curtis was a good party man and eventually became Republican majority leader in 1924. In 1928, Curtis, as a Kansas "favorite son," opposed the nomination of Herbert Hoover at the Republican convention. Hoover won the nomination, however, and the convention picked Curtis as his running mate. They defeated the Democrats headed by Al Smith.

Curtis was sixty-nine when he entered the office and many considered him mediocre and thought it appropriate that he was vice-president when the musical *Of Thee I Sing* appeared on Broadway. The play poked fun at a vice-president named Alexander Throttlebottom, a name that has become synonymous with ineffectual, unimportant vice-presidents.

Hoover and Curtis were renominated in 1932 but were defeated by Franklin D. Roosevelt and John Nance Garner. Curtis retired to practice law in Washington, D.C., where he died in 1936.

John Nance Garner, 1933–1941

John Nance Garner thought that next to being president, the Speaker of the House was the most powerful job in Washington. He did not want to be vice-president, and when Franklin Roosevelt asked him to be his running mate in 1932, he made a remark that is now part of our history books. "The vice-presidency is not worth a warm bucket of spit," said Garner.

Garner was born in a log cabin in Red River County, Texas, in 1868. He received little formal education, and although admitted to Vanderbilt University, he was forced to leave after one year because he was not prepared for college work. He studied law in Clarksville, Texas, and was admitted to the bar in 1890. His doctor said he needed to move to a dry climate for his health, so he opened a law practice in Uvalde, Texas. In 1902, he was elected to Congress, where he served for thirty years. In 1931, he achieved his lifelong ambition when he became Speaker of the House. But he only served in that office one year. At the 1932 Democratic convention, the party was deadlocked over the nomination of Franklin D. Roosevelt, who did not have enough votes for the presidential nomination. Garner controlled the Texas and California delegations and was himself a candidate for the presidency. When he realized he could not get the nomination, he swung his votes to Roosevelt. But Garner's backers refused to vote for FDR unless Garner was made the vice-presidential candidate. Garner preferred to remain Speaker of the House, but he went along out of loyalty to the party.

Roosevelt and Garner defeated Hoover and Curtis, and soon, in an effort to bring some relief to the depression-torn country, Garner was helping Roosevelt push his revolutionary New Deal legislation through Congress. He also attended many cabinet meetings and worked closely with Roosevelt. They were re-elected by a landslide in 1936, but, in his second term, Garner had many serious disagreements with Roosevelt. Above all, he did not approve of the president's effort to pack the Supreme Court with six new liberal justices, refusing to help push the necessary legislation in Congress. He also broke with Roosevelt in the mid-term elections of 1938, when Roosevelt tried to intervene in state elections to defeat the Democratic senators who had voted against the Supreme Court packing bill. Ultimately, he disagreed with Roosevelt's decision to run for a third term in 1940. Garner himself was a candidate for president at the convention, but the Democrats renominated Roosevelt and chose Henry Wallace as his running mate. They were elected.

After retiring from office, Garner returned to Texas and lived a quiet life until his death at the age of ninety-eight in 1967.

Henry A. Wallace, 1941–1945

Henry A. Wallace was born on a farm in Iowa in 1888. His father, Henry C. Wallace, was a farmer and editor who had been secretary of agriculture in the administrations of Presidents Harding and Coolidge. The son graduated from Iowa State College in 1910 and joined the family magazine, *Wallace's Farmer*. He became an expert on farm pricing and corn farming, eventually developing a hybrid corn, which he sold through his own company.

In 1928, he shifted from his father's party to the Democrats and became active in farm politics. President Roosevelt appointed him secretary of agriculture in 1933, and Wallace became the principal advocate and organizer of the New Deal's farm programs during the depression. Wallace was considered something of a radical and many Democrats were afraid of him. However, he was popular with the farmers, and in 1940 Roosevelt picked him to run as vice-president when he sought an historic third term.

With the nation heading into a world war, Roosevelt gave his new vice-president more and more executive responsibilities. Wallace participated in cabinet meetings and was given numerous special assignments, which made him the most active and powerful vice-president up to that time.

However, in exercising this power he made political enemies. And with Roosevelt obviously tired and worn out from his wartime duties, opposition arose to Wallace as his running mate in 1944. As a result, Wallace was passed over for the vice-presidential nomination at the 1944 convention after months of political intrigue among Roosevelt's political supporters. Many were considered for the job, but it finally went to Senator Harry S. Truman of Missouri.

After Roosevelt was re-elected for his fourth term in 1944, he appointed Wallace secretary of commerce. But Wallace was forced to resign that post in 1946 when he criticized President Truman's "get tough" policy toward Russia. Two years later, he became a candidate for president on the Progressive party ticket. When he was defeated, he broke with the Progressive party and retired to a farm in upstate New York to devote the remainder of his life to agriculture. He died in 1965 at the age of seventy-seven.

Alben W. Barkley, 1949–1953

Alben W. Barkley was seventy-one when inaugurated to the vice-presidency, the oldest man ever to hold the office. He was also the only vice-president ever to get married while in office.

Barkley was born in a log cabin in Graves County, Kentucky, in 1877. He graduated from Marvin College in Kentucky in 1897 after attending Emory College briefly. He then worked as a law clerk to finance his tuition at the University of Virginia Law School. After being admitted to the bar in 1901, he began practicing law in Paducah, Kentucky.

He also became active in local Democratic politics, serving as county prosecuting attorney and judge of the county court before being elected to the U.S. House of Representatives in 1912. He served seven terms in the House before being elected to the Senate in 1926. His popularity in the Senate led to his being elected Senate majority leader in 1937. He was an early supporter of the New Deal and played an important role in guiding Roosevelt's legislation through the Senate. He also was an important and popular party worker, giving the keynote speeches at the conventions of 1932, 1936, and 1948, and holding important convention posts in 1940, 1944, and 1948.

In 1948, the Democrats picked Barkley to run as their vice-presidential candidate after President Truman had failed in his efforts to persuade Justice William O. Douglas to run. Truman, thinking Barkley was happy in the Senate, was surprised to learn that he was interested in the vice-presidency. Barkley made the first crosscountry campaign by airplane, while Truman crossed the country by train, speaking at his famous "whistle stops." They upset the Republicans in a dramatic close election.

Barkley was one of the most popular vice-presidents ever to hold the vice-presidency. He became known as "Veep" when he told a news conference that was what his grandson called him; he was married for a second time while in office. Truman had decided that Barkley would become a "working vice-president" and invited him to sit in on cabinet meetings and persuaded Congress to pass a law making the vice-president a member of the National Security Council.

In 1952, Barkley was a candidate for the presidency after Truman announced that he would not run. However, he withdrew from the race after learning that organized labor, which traditionally makes up a large part of the Democratic voting block, opposed him because of his age (seventy-five). In 1954, he was elected senator from Kentucky, but he only served in office two years. He died while giving a speech at the University of Virginia. His last words were: "I would rather be a servant in the House of the Lord than to sit in the seats of the mighty."

Hubert H. Humphrey, 1965–1969

Hubert H. Humphrey was born in Wallace, South Dakota, in 1911. His father, a pharmacist, owned a drugstore, and as a boy he worked in the store and planned to become a pharmacist. After graduating from the Denver College of Pharmacy in 1933, he became a registered pharmacist in Huron, South Dakota. However, Humphrey became interested in politics and in 1937 he entered the University of Minnesota. After graduation in 1939 he attended Louisiana State University and received a master's degree in political science in 1940.

During the war, he returned to Minnesota where he taught at Macalester College in St. Paul and served in a number of civilian war jobs. In 1944, he was state campaign director for the Roosevelt presidential campaign, and during this period he was instrumental in merging the Democratic and Farm Labor parties into the DFL, which dominated Minnesota politics for many years. In 1945, he was elected mayor of Minneapolis, and after serving two terms, he decided to run for the Senate. At the Democratic convention in 1948, he gained national fame by forcing the convention to adopt a strong civil rights platform, which led to the "Dixiecrat" revolt from the party and the nomination of their own candidate for the presidency. Humphrey's move was credited with winning the black vote for Harry Truman in 1948.

Humphrey was elected to the Senate in 1949, the same year Lyndon Johnson entered the Senate. Johnson and Humphrey became good friends and both emerged as powerful Democratic leaders in the Senate. Humphrey was re-elected in 1954 and 1960, and during his years in the Senate he worked diligently to pass many landmark bills, including legislation on civil rights, Medicare, the Peace Corps, Social Security, the Job Corps, Headstart, housing and urban development, and food stamps. The Humphrey-Durham Drug Act and the Humphrey-Hawkins Full Employment Bill are testimonials to his legislative achievements.

He also played an important role in the Senate Foreign Relations Committee and in 1956 was appointed by President Eisenhower as U.S. delegate to the United Nations General Assembly.

Humphrey was an inspiring orator and a leader of the liberal wing of the Democratic party. He had hoped to be the party's vice-presidential candidate in 1956, but the convention chose Senator Estes Kefauver of Tennessee instead. In 1960, he tried to win the party's presidential nomination but lost to Senator John F. Kennedy of Massachusetts, who chose Lyndon Johnson as his running mate. Humphrey campaigned tirelessly for their election. In 1964, Lyndon Johnson, who had become president after the assassination of John F. Kennedy, chose Humphrey as his running mate. They defeated Republican Senator Barry Goldwater and Congressman William Miller, in one of the most decisive victories in American history.

When Johnson picked Humphrey, he said that his vice-president would be one of the most active in American history. And he was right. Johnson delegated to Humphrey numerous responsibilities at home and abroad, and, in his four years in office, Humphrey expanded the power and responsibilities of the office beyond that of any prior vice-president. And for brief periods, when President Johnson was hospitalized, Vice-President Humphrey stood ready and fully authorized (under the Twenty-fifth Amendment enacted in 1967) to take over the powers of the presidency.

However, Humphrey realized that his primary responsibility was loyalty to the president and that his power had its limitations. "There are no Humphrey policies, no Humphrey programs. I'm a close adviser and member of the team." He also said: "The vice-president will be and is what the president wants him to be . . . a loyal, faithful friend and servant."

Humphrey's loyalty also included his support of Johnson's policy on the Vietnam War at a time when the country was turning against the war. This hurt Humphrey considerably. In 1964, when Johnson chose not to run again, Senator Robert F. Kennedy, Eugene McCarthy, and Vice-President Humphrey became the principal Democratic contenders for the presidential nomination. After Robert Kennedy was assassinated in California in June, Humphrey emerged as the leading contender and was nominated the following month at the Democratic convention. He chose Senator Edmund Muskie of Maine as his running mate. By the end of the campaign, Humphrey had begun to pull away from Johnson's war policies and the polls showed a trend in his direction. But it was too late. Humphrey and Muskie were defeated by Richard Nixon and Spiro Agnew in one of the closest elections in American history.

After leaving the vice-presidency, Humphrey returned to Minnesota to teach at Macalester College and the University of Minnesota. He was re-elected to the Senate in 1970 and was a candidate for the Democratic presidential nomination again in 1972. However, the Democrats nominated Senator George McGovern who was defeated by incumbent Richard Nixon. Humphrey died of cancer in 1978 at the age of sixty-six.

Spiro T. Agnew, 1969–1973

Spiro T. Agnew was the only vice-president forced to resign his office. He was born in Baltimore, Maryland, in 1918, the son of Greek immigrants. He attended public schools before entering Johns Hopkins University in Baltimore, where he studied for three years. Then he transferred to the Baltimore Law School, which he attended at night while working in the daytime for insurance companies. During World War II, he left law school to serve in France and Germany and was awarded the Bronze Star. In the postwar years he returned to law school and graduated in 1947.

After he was admitted to the bar, he moved to suburban Towson, Maryland, and began practicing law. He soon gained a local reputation as a specialist in labor cases. He also switched from the Democratic to the Republican party. In 1957, he was appointed to the Zoning Board in Baltimore County and in 1962 became the first Republican since the Civil War to be elected executive of Baltimore County. In 1966, he ran for governor of Maryland and won, getting the votes of most liberals and blacks because his opponent was an outspoken racist. But after Baltimore suffered serious race riots early in 1968, he became more conservative and began to denounce activist leaders and student protesters. He became a leading advocate for "law and order."

Agnew was a supporter of Nelson Rockefeller for the Republican presidential nomination in 1968, but when Rockefeller withdrew, he shifted his support to Richard Nixon and placed his name in nomination at the Republican convention. When Nixon received the nomination, he chose Agnew, virtually unknown outside the state of Maryland, as his vice-presidential running mate. They were elected, although Agnew hurt the ticket and gained national notoriety by referring to newsmen of Japanese descent as "fat Japs" and describing American Poles as "Polacks."

As vice-president, Agnew was mostly active in the political area and traveled around the country giving conservative speeches for the administration. He gained attention for his attacks on newsmen, describing them as "nabobs of negativism." He and Nixon were re-elected in 1972, but in 1973 it became known that Agnew had been involved in some illegal financial deals while governor of Maryland. He was indicted by a grand jury and forced to resign from office after pleading "no contest" to charges of federal income tax violations. He was fined but did not have to serve a jail sentence.

After his resignation, he returned to private life and has been representing the business interests of various foreign countries.

Nelson A. Rockefeller, 1974–1977

Nelson A. Rockefeller was born in Bar Harbor, Maine, in 1908.
He was the grandson of John D. Rockefeller, one of the richest men
of his era, who made his fortune in the oil business. Like Franklin

Roosevelt, Nelson Rockefeller dreamed of being president from the time he was a boy. He attended Lincoln High School in New York and then Dartmouth College, from which he graduated in 1930. He worked in various offices in his family's business before entering public service. During World War II, he was assistant secretary of state, where he became an expert in Latin American affairs. In 1950, he was named head of the International Development Board, which was part of the foreign aid program. Rockefeller was a Republican, and after the election of General Dwight D. Eisenhower in 1952, he was appointed head of the President's Advisory Committee on Government Organization. A year later, he was made undersecretary of the Department of Health, Education and Welfare.

In 1956, Rockefeller returned to New York State to become involved in state affairs and Republican politics. He ran for governor of New York in 1958 and won an impressive victory in a year when Democrats were winning almost everywhere else. He was re-elected governor in 1962, 1966, and 1970. Although criticized for spending too much money, he was an extremely popular governor, giving New York a liberal government for fourteen years. During this time, Rockefeller was also pursuing his ambition to be president. In 1960, he actively campaigned for the Republican presidential nomination, but lost to Richard Nixon. However, he was instrumental in liberalizing the Republican platform. Four years later, he tried for the nomination again, but lost to the conservative Barry Goldwater. Rockefeller failed again in 1968, when the Republicans nominated Richard Nixon for the second time. In 1973, he resigned from the governorship of New York to give more time, it was said, to his efforts to win the Republican presidential nomination in 1976.

In 1974, when Vice-President Gerald Ford became president after the resignation of President Nixon, Ford had to pick a replacement, as decreed in the Twenty-fifth Amendment to the Constitution. President Ford chose Nelson Rockefeller for the vice-presidency, and he was confirmed by the House and the Senate.

Rockefeller was in office a little more than a year. He always had strong opposition from Republican conservatives who felt Rockefeller was a Democrat in disguise. Pressure from the conservatives forced Rockefeller not to be a candidate for the vice-presidency again in 1976, and when President Ford was renominated, the convention chose Senator Robert Dole of Kansas as his running mate. They were defeated by Jimmy Carter and Walter Mondale. After he left the vice-presidency, Rockefeller retired from politics to devote his time to art collecting. He died in 1978.

Walter F. Mondale, 1977–1981

Walter F. Mondale was born in Ceylon, Minnesota, in 1928. His father was a Methodist minister and his mother a music teacher. He spent his boyhood in the small towns of Minnesota, attending public

115

schools in Ceylon, Heron Lake, and Elmore. He took an early interest in politics. While attending Macalester College in St. Paul, he helped manage Hubert Humphrey's first campaign for the Senate in 1948.

In 1949, Mondale took a year off from school to work in Washington, D.C., then he returned to the University of Minnesota for his bachelor's degree in political science. After two years in the army during the Korean War, he earned his law degree at the University of Minnesota in 1956.

For the next four years, Mondale practiced law in Minneapolis, at the same time continuing his active interest in politics. In 1960, Governor Orville Freeman appointed him to fill a vacancy in the office of state attorney general. Two years later, he was elected to the office and served in it until 1964, when Governor Karl Rolvaag appointed him to fill the U.S. Senate seat created by Senator Hubert Humphrey's election to the vice-presidency. He was elected to the Senate in 1966 and 1972. He quickly became a hard-working member of the Senate Democratic team, serving on the Finance, Labor and Public Welfare, and Budget committees and several select committees including Governmental Operations, Equal Educational Opportunity, Nutrition and Human Needs and Aging, Children and Youth, and Social Security Financing.

In his eleven years in the Senate, Mondale also became one of the leading spokesmen for the liberal wing of the Democratic party. In this role, he had considerable support for the presidential candidacy in 1976. However, after a committee appointed by him studied the situation for several months in 1974, Mondale called a press conference to announce that he had decided "not to be a candidate for the Democratic presidential nomination in 1976." While there were many reasons that could be given, Mondale explained, "Basically, I found that I did not have the overwhelming desire to be president, which is essential for the kind of campaigning that is required." To seek the presidency, Mondale said he would have to reduce his role in the Senate and his ability to serve Minnesota, which he did not want to do.

The decision was a blow to the liberal Democrats, most of whom were backing him for the presidency. But they were rewarded two years later when the former governor of Georgia, Jimmy Carter, who won the Democratic presidential nomination, picked Mondale as his running mate. It was a move designed to balance the ticket with a northern liberal, someone experienced in the political ways of Washington. Carter and Mondale defeated President Gerald Ford and Senator Robert Dole in the 1976 election.

As vice-president, Mondale, with President Carter's encouragement and endorsement, carried the concept of a substantive vice-president into many areas of executive responsibility. One study, made by the *National Journal* approximately halfway through Mondale's term, concluded that he "is the most active and visible vice-president of modern times," an assessment with which most students of the vice-presidency agreed. Throughout his four years in office, Mondale continued to meet regularly with the president and the Cabinet. And he was continually consulted by Jimmy Carter and brought into the decision-making process on most major issues facing his Administration.

George Bush, 1981–

George Bush, the present vice-president of the United States, was born in 1924 in Milton, Massachusetts. He graduated from Andover Academy in 1942 and enlisted in the U.S. Navy, becoming at age

118

18 the youngest commissioned pilot in the navy at that time. During World War II, he saw service as a carrier pilot in the Pacific theater, winning three air medals and the Distinguished Flying Cross.

After the war, he attended Yale University, where he captained the baseball team and majored in economics. He graduated a Phi Beta Kappa in 1948. An early interest in politics was inspired, in part, by his father, Prescott Bush, who represented Connecticut in the U.S. Senate from 1952 to 1962.

When Bush graduated from Yale, he went to work as a supply salesman in the oil tools division of Dresser industries, which took him to West Texas and California. In 1951, he cofounded the Bush-Overby Development Company, a small firm that put together deals for exploratory oil-drilling. Two years later, he started the Zapata Petroleum Company, named after the movie, "Viva Zapata." In 1954, he became cofounder and president of the Zapata Off-Shore Company, which built the first off-shore drilling equipment. Today, much of the offshore oil produced around the world is drilled for by the rigs Bush's company pioneered.

Having become a successful and financially independent business-man by his early 30s, Bush decided to follow his father's footsteps and go into politics. In 1966, he was elected to the U.S. House of Representatives from the 7th district of Texas. He served two terms in the House, and in 1970 he ran for a Texas senate seat and was defeated. However, his political career was continued when President Nixon appointed him Ambassador to the United Nations, a post he held from 1971 to 1973. Then he served with acknowledged discretion as chairman of the Republican National Committee during the dark days of the Watergate scandals—from January 1973 to September 1974. In October of 1974, President Ford appointed him chief of the U.S. Liaison Office in the People's Republic of China. Then he was appointed Director of the Central Intelligence Agency and remained in that job until January 1977.

With his broad experience in government, Bush felt that he was ready to seek the presidency, and in 1980 he entered a number of primaries as a presidential candidate representing the moderate wing of the Republican party. He was defeated by Ronald Reagan, but then, much to Bush's surprise, Reagan chose him as his running mate at the 1980 Republican convention in Detroit. Reagan and Bush defeated Carter and Mondale, and Bush was sworn in as the nation's forty-third vice president on January 20, 1980.

"I May Be Everything"

It was the first vice-president, John Adams, who made the often quoted remark: "I am vice-president. In this I am nothing. But I may be everything."

The men we have discussed in this chapter never became "everything" (although Walter Mondale and George Bush could conceivably someday be President). Consequently, they have been consigned to history as "nothing." They are, or will be, as forgotten as Hannibal Hamlin, and about the most significant thing you can say about them collectively is that many of them started out their careers studying law. Of the forty-three vice-presidents in our history, thirty were lawyers. Two of the non-lawyers—Theodore Roosevelt and Schuyler Colfax—studied law for a while.

It is often stressed that the only man in history actually to seek the vice-presidency was James Polk, and he was nominated for the presidency instead. But it is also significant to note that only two men in history who were nominated for the office actually turned it down—Senator Silas Wright of New York in 1844 and Governor Frank Lowden of Illinois in 1924. Of course, many vice-presidential candidates accepted the nomination only out of loyalty to their party. For example, when President Roosevelt was told that Senator Harry Truman did not want the vice-presidential nomination in 1944, FDR said: "You tell him that if he wants to break up the Democratic party in the middle of a war, that's his responsibility." Truman's response was: "Well, if that's the situation, I have to say yes." And in 1980, former President Gerald Ford, although never actually nominated, turned down Ronald Reagan's offer of the vice-presidency when Reagan would not accept Ford's concept of a "copresident." As it turned out, in addition to not wanting a "copresident," Reagan apparently had concluded that the modern vice-president had become, perhaps, too active.

It is also true that, throughout our history, many presidential hopefuls have settled for the vice-presidency when it became apparent they could not have the top spot. Senator Lyndon Johnson, the powerful majority leader of the Senate, completely surprised his supporters when he accepted the vice-presidential nomination in 1960. Nelson Rockefeller consented to be Ford's vice-president in 1974 after years of seeking the presidency. "I never wanted to be vice-president of anything," he said. And in 1980, George Bush accepted the vice-presidency after an unsuccessful bid for the presidency.

The vice-presidency of the United States has gradually emerged as one of the most powerful jobs in government. It is no longer considered "a disgrace . . . like writing anonymous letters," as Peter Finley Dunne once described it. "I may have more influence in government [as vice-president] than I ever had in the Senate because of my role with the president," said Vice-President Mondale. The truth is that the power and influence of the vice-presidency is no more or less than the president wants it to be. But in recent years, more and more presidents have been granting their vice-presidents increased powers and responsibilities. Just how this came about is examined in the following chapter.

Vice-President George Bush with President Ronald Reagan. Bush stresses that his influence in the Reagan Administration will depend primarily on the extent to which he can win the president's confidence.   *Cynthia Johnson/The White House*

The Making
of the Vice-President:
1789–1981

The creation of the office of vice-presidency was almost an afterthought of the Constitutional Convention. It primarily grew out of two concerns of the delegates: (1) if the Senate exercised the powers of the presidency during the period of a special election called to fill a vacancy in the office, this would give too much power to the legislative branch, and (2) what was the best method of choosing a president if the office was vacated.

Both of these problems were resolved by a plan that called for the presidential college to elect two men for the executive branch. The one who received the most votes would be president; the one who received the next highest total would be vice-president. And the vice-president would accept the powers and duties of the chief executive if anything happened to incapacitate him. His only other duty would be to preside over the Senate, voting only if there were a tie. Three delegates to the convention opposed the office of vice-president, but it did emerge in the final draft of the Constitution. This method of choosing our two top executives presented no problems in the first two elections, because George Washington was clearly the majority choice of the electoral college and John Adams was the second choice, and he was elected vice-president.

However, problems began to develop in the third presidential election, in 1796. John Adams, a Federalist, opposed Thomas Jefferson, head of the anti-Federalists, or Democratic-Republicans. Thomas Pinckney was the Federalist's candidate for vice-president, and the Democratic-Republicans supported Aaron Burr for that office. It appeared that the Federalists had won the election, but political maneuvering in the electoral college resulted in Adams's being elected president and Thomas Jefferson, instead of Pinckney, vice-president. This created problems for the country; it was as if a Republican president and a Democratic vice-president had been elected at the same time.

No crisis resulted, but the presidential election four years later, in 1800, created another problem. The candidates were the same—Adams and Pinckney vs. Jefferson and Burr—except that Thomas Pinckney's brother, Charles, was now the Federalist's choice for vice-president. This time, the Democratic-Republicans won, but again, political manipulating in the electoral college resulted in a confused situation. Jefferson and Burr each received seventy-three votes, so there was, in effect, a tie for the presidency. However, Burr refused the vice-presidency, so the tie had to be broken in the House of Representatives, where each state had one vote. After thirty-six ballots, Jefferson won the majority of votes, but the confusion and bitterness caused by the disputed election prompted the Congress to enact the Twelfth Amendment to the Constitution, which called for separate ballots for the president and vice-president. There could still be a tie in the electoral college (which would, as before, be settled in the House), but it made sure that two candidates for the presidency would never again end up serving as president and vice-president.

The confusion was eliminated, but the Twelfth Amendment also lowered the prestige of the vice-president. No longer would he be the second most capable and prominent man running for president. Now he would be somebody picked by his party to serve only as

Thomas Jefferson took part in two disputed elections, leading to the ratification of the Twelfth Amendment to the Constitution, which clarified rules concerning the election of the president and vice-president. *Library of Congress*

the vice-presidential candidate, someone to assume leadership if something happened to the president.

The first man to become vice-president under the new provisions of the Twelfth Amendment was George Clinton in 1804. He was supported by the northern Democrats who opposed the "Virginia dynasty" represented by Thomas Jefferson, the party's presidential candidate. The Virginians had no objection to Clinton. They wanted a northerner to help win the election and they knew Clinton, who was sixty-five years old, would be too old in 1808 to be a serious presidential candidate. Thus, a precedent was established that dominated American politics well into the twentieth century: vice-presidential candidates were picked for political considerations, rather than on their own qualifications to serve as president. It also meant that from 1804 until the middle of the twentieth century, most—but not all—of our vice-presidential candidates have been men of lesser stature than the men who were nominated for the presidency.

The next major landmark in the development of the vice-presidency occurred in 1841, when President William Harrison became the first president to die in office. It was assumed by scholars and political experts, including former President John Quincy Adams, that the vice-president—John Tyler—would only become an "acting president," not the real president, until the next election in 1844. They were even opposed to Tyler's occupancy of the White House or his being paid a president's salary. Tyler would not accept that decision. He moved into the White House, took the oath of office as president, and assumed all the president's constitutional powers. This established the precedent that the vice-president would succeed to the presidency on the death of the president, and it has never been challenged. Constitutional scholars eventually decided that Adams's interpretation was right, but it was too late—the precedent had already been set.

There still remained, however, the question of what happened when the president became disabled and could not carry out his duties.

Chester A. Arthur (here seen with a friend on his estate in New York) remained at his home during the prolonged incapacitation of President James Garfield before the president died from an assassin's bullet. *Library of Congress*

During the eighty days President James Garfield was incapacitated after he was shot by an assassin in 1881, Vice-President Chester A. Arthur decided to make no move to act for the disabled president. He remained in seclusion in New York and communicated with Secretary of State James G. Blaine in Washington, who gave him reports on the president's condition. Garfield eventually died and Arthur assumed the presidency without opposition.

The problem of presidential disability assumed even greater proportions during Woodrow Wilson's second administration, when he suffered a nervous breakdown and was incapacitated for nearly six months. Vice-President Thomas Riley Marshall faced an agonizing dilemma: should he assume responsibilities for a job he felt unqualified to fill or should he let the situation drift on with the country apparently being governed by Mrs. Wilson? Marshall decided to do nothing, telling his wife that a rash move might "throw the country into civil war." Wilson eventually recovered, and although four bills were introduced in the Congress to clarify what to do when a president becomes dis-

Vice-President Thomas R. Marshall, substituting for President Wilson, throws out the first ball at the opening of the 1920 baseball season.   *Library of Congress*

abled, they were never passed and the question was soon forgotten. However, Wilson's illness did remind the country and the politicians of the necessity of electing capable men to the vice-presidency.

The disability question arose again in the administrations of General Dwight D. Eisenhower (when the president suffered at separate times a heart attack and a mild stroke and underwent surgery) and Lyndon B. Johnson (when he suffered a heart attack and also had to undergo gall bladder surgery). After his stroke, President Eisenhower urged Congress to do something about the disability question. When Congress failed to act, he worked out an agreement himself with Vice-President Nixon, which was made public, setting forth the conditions under which the vice-president would take over the responsibilities of the president and how the president would resume them if he could. Finally, in 1965, partly as a result of President Johnson's illness, Congress

Vice-President Nixon (right) shaking hands with President Eisenhower in 1955 after a goodwill trip to Asia. *The Dwight D. Eisenhower Library*

Calvin Coolidge was the first vice-president since John Adams to sit regularly with the president's cabinet. Coolidge (at end of table) poses in a formal photograph with President Warren G. Harding's cabinet in 1921. President Harding is at the head of the table.   *Library of Congress*

passed the Bayh Amendment, which, when ratified by three-fourths of the states in 1967, became the Twenty-fifth Amendment to the Constitution. It states that the vice-president, acting with a majority of the president's cabinet or "of such other body as Congress may by law provide," will transmit to the Senate a written statement that the president is no longer able to discharge the duties and powers of his office; in which case the vice-president will assume the office of the presidency until the vice-president and the majority of the cabinet, or other body, are satisfied that the president is capable of resuming the powers and responsibilities of office. After 179 years of confusion and uncertainty, the question of what happens when the president becomes incapacitated was resolved.

130

Another aspect of the vice-presidency that took decades to clarify was the question of his relationship to the president's cabinet and the executive branch of government. In 1791, President Washington invited Vice-President Adams to attend cabinet meetings. But when Adams became president, his vice-president—Thomas Jefferson—declined to sit in the cabinet, saying: "I consider my office as constitutionally confined to legislative functions, and that I could not take any part whatever in executive consultations." As a result, no vice-president attended a cabinet meeting until World War I.

In 1918, when President Wilson went to Paris to attend the peace conference, he asked Vice-President Marshall to preside over cabinet meetings. But when Wilson returned, Marshall was again excluded from the meetings. President Warren Harding asked Vice-President Coolidge to attend cabinet meetings, but Coolidge's vice-president—Charles Dawes—said he would not attend the meetings because it might set a precedent for the future, when a president might have a vice-president he did not want to sit with the cabinet. However, the precedent was set once and for all by Franklin Roosevelt, who invited his vice-presidents to attend cabinet meetings. And President Eisenhower asked Vice-President Nixon to preside over the cabinet meetings in his absence. Prior to that, the secretary of state traditionally presided at the cabinet meetings in the president's absence.

However, the elevation of the vice-presidency was a long time coming. Over most of the nineteenth century, the office was held in low esteem by politicians and voters alike. Only one man, Martin Van Buren, was ever elected directly from the vice-presidency to the presidency. And, in 1840, Van Buren participated in an election that marked the lowest point in the vice-presidency. When the Democratic convention could not agree on a running mate for Van Buren, he ran in the campaign without one. The electoral college would have been free to vote for anyone it chose. But, as it turned out, it did not matter, because Van Buren was defeated. By the end of the century,

At the end of the nineteenth century, the vice-presidency was still held in such low esteem that Vice-President Theodore Roosevelt, pictured here (right) with President William McKinley, suggested the office be abolished. *Library of Congress*

the office was so unpopular that Theodore Roosevelt suggested it be abolished. He said it was "not a steppingstone to anything but oblivion," and the more he thought about it, he said, the more he would rather be anything—even a professor of history—than vice-president. He accepted the post, however, and was soon in the White House as president.

The turning point in the evolution of the vice-presidency occurred in the administration of Franklin D. Roosevelt. Partly because of his own physical handicaps and partly because of the many problems facing the country during his administration (first the depression and then World War II), Roosevelt gave his vice-presidents increasing responsibilities. Vice-President Garner was an active participant in Roosevelt's government; he attended cabinet meetings and provided important advice and leadership in pushing Roosevelt's New Deal

The turning point in the vice-presidency came in the administration of Franklin D. Roosevelt, whose three vice-presidents were given steadily increasing powers. His first vice-president was John Nance Garner, shown above. *Library of Congress*

legislation through Congress. In 1935, Garner became the first vice-president in history to visit a foreign country on official business, when he represented the United States at the inauguration of President Manuel Quezon of the Philippines. And during World War II, Roosevelt made Vice-President Wallace head of the Board of Economic Warfare and sought his advice on policy-making in several areas. He also sent Wallace on a goodwill tour of Latin America in 1943.

Roosevelt's final vice-president was Harry Truman who, after less than three months in office, was suddenly thrust into the White House. When he took the oath of office, he told the newspapermen: "Boys, if you ever pray, pray for me now. I don't know whether you fellows ever had a load of hay fall on you, but when they told me yesterday what had happened, I felt like the moon, the stars, and all the planets had fallen on me."

FDR's third vice-president, Harry S. Truman, was not in office long enough to be given many responsibilities. In less than three months after his inauguration, he became president. In this photo, Vice-President-elect Truman (center) and Vice-President Henry Wallace (right) return to Washington with President Roosevelt after the 1944 election.
Abbie Rowe/The Harry S. Truman Library

Once again, the country was reminded that the vice-president, at any moment, could suddenly become president. And since Truman's presidency, the office of vice-president has steadily increased in importance and responsibility. Truman made every effort to bring his vice-president into the affairs of his administration and tried in other ways to enhance the office, such as urging Congress to create a special flag and seal for the vice-president. In 1949, Congress, at President Truman's urging, made him a member of the National Security Council. And in 1954 President Eisenhower directed that the vice-president, rather than the secretary of state, preside over National Security Council meetings in the president's absence. Each president after Truman continued to increase the power and responsibilities of the vice-president, and events soon made it appear that the vice-presidency had become the second most important office in the country. The assassination of President John F. Kennedy suddenly made Vice-President Lyndon B. Johnson president. And ten years later, the corruption and scandal in the Nixon-Agnew administration created chaos in the executive branch of the government. In 1973, Vice-President Spiro Agnew was forced to resign because of scandal and he was replaced by Congressman Gerald R. Ford. Then Nixon himself was forced to resign because of the Watergate scandals and Ford became president. President Ford picked former New York Governor Nelson Rockefeller as vice-president, and Rockefeller narrowly missed becoming president when assassination attempts on President Ford's life failed.

The successful and unsuccessful attempts to assassinate the president in recent years dramatized the importance of the vice-presidency in ways that have seldom been discussed. Now, perhaps more than ever, it is essential to have a vice-president in office who is politically loyal to the president, one who is informed on matters of state and ready to step in and take charge if anything happens to the man in the White House. There might be even more assassination attempts if it were thought that by removing the president there would be a new election or it would bring into office a man who held views different from the president's. The fact that there is a man already in office prepared to serve until the next presidential election and who can be counted on to carry out the president's policies should discourage presidential assassinations.

As a result of the events of the last thirty-nine years, by the time President Ronald Reagan and Vice-President George Bush took office in 1981, the vice-president's role in government was vastly different from what it was in 1789.

Vice-President Nixon talks with Senator John F. Kennedy about Allen Drury's *Advise and Consent,* a 1959 best-selling book about Washington politics. *The National Archives*

The vice-president is sworn in at the same time as the president, shortly after noon on January 20, in the year following a presidential election. Oddly enough, the Twenty-second Amendment, which limits the president to two terms in office, places no restrictions on the vice-president. He can serve as many terms in office as he can be elected. Here Vice-President Humphrey is sworn in by Speaker of the House John W. McCormack in 1965. Behind Humphrey is President Lyndon B. Johnson.

President Kennedy's vice-president, Lyndon B. Johnson, talking with Kennedy a month before the president was assassinated, says the president realized the vice-presidency was a difficult job "and did everything he could to give it substance."

The vice-president en route to Berlin in 1961; to his left is General Lucius Clay.

The Lyndon B. Johnson Library

Vice-President Johnson rides in a motorcade during a 1962 visit to Naples, Italy, a trip that also took him on a goodwill tour of the Middle East.

United States Information Service

Johnson, on far left, at 1962 cabinet meeting.

Hubert Humphrey, as vice-president, is in Birmingham, Alabama, in 1967, talking with high school students at a football game.

Vice-President Humphrey visits American troops at the 38th Parallel in Korea.

President Nixon also gave his vice-president, Spiro Agnew, many assignments that drew the vice-president into active participation in the Nixon administration. Here, Agnew meets at Camp David in 1972 with President Nixon and Secretary of State Henry Kissinger.

Vice-President Agnew discusses a legislative problem in his Senate office in 1969 with former Maryland senator, Joseph R. Tydings. *Paul Conklin*

Although he was in office less than a year, Gerald Ford continued the tradition of a modern activist vice-president. At his hearing before Congress, after President Nixon picked him to replace Spiro Agnew, Ford was asked how partisan he would be as vice-president. He replied that he would be just as partisan as his predecessors, Vice-Presidents Truman, Johnson, and Humphrey. It was a good answer, because all vice-presidents are politically partisan, often more so, at least in public, than the president under whom they serve. Vice-President Ford here speaks to the 1974 National Urban League Conference. *Thomas/The National Archives*

Vice-President Ford signs a joint revenue-sharing agreement with Governor William
Milliken of Michigan in 1974.   *Thomas/The National Archives*

Vice-President Nelson A. Rockefeller speaks to the Congressional Black Caucus Fo-
rum in the Rayburn House Office Building.   *Jack Kightlinger*

Vice-President Rockefeller meets with members of the Japanese Diet visiting the U.S.

One of the most dramatic and moving moments in the history of the vice-presidency occurred in January 1978 at the memorial service for the late Senator Hubert Humphrey—the thirty-eighth vice-president of the United States. His old friend and protégé, Vice-President Walter F. Mondale, spoke about Humphrey as he lay in state in the rotunda of the Capitol. Humphrey had always wanted to be president, but Mondale said that "even though he failed to realize his greatest goal, he achieved something much more rare and valuable than the nation's highest office. He became the country's conscience. . . .

"He taught us all how to hope and how to love, how to win and how to lose, he taught us how to live and, finally, he taught us how to die." *Robert McNeely/*
The White House

George Bush in a near-empty office in his early days as vice-president. "The Mondale Model" of the vice-presidency is the one he wants to emulate. *Cynthia Johnson/ The White House*

Vice-President Walter F. Mondale leaves the Capitol after exercising his one official duty—presiding over the Senate of the United States, which a vice-president does only rarely. With him are Jim Johnson (behind Mondale on left), his executive assistant, and Al Eisele (right), his press secretary. *Robert McNeely/The White House*

5

The Vice-Presidency Today

It is apparent from our study of the vice-presidency that the power and influence of the vice-president in any administration depends solely on how much the president chooses to give him. And since the 1930s, our presidents have gradually increased this power, although until Carter, no presidents actually took their vice-presidents into the decision-making process. But over the years, presidents Truman, Eisenhower, Kennedy, Johnson, Nixon, and Ford all gave their vice-presidents increasing responsibilities.

President Jimmy Carter, however, went further than his predecessors in bringing his vice-president into the process of running the government. When he picked Senator Walter Mondale as his running mate, he said he planned to give his vice-president more power, influence, and responsibility than any previous vice-president in history. Many students of government doubted Carter really meant this, which prompted the *Washington Post* to assign Pulitzer Prize winning correspondent David Broder to assess Vice-President Mondale's role in the Carter administration. After following the vice-president in his daily activities for a week, Broder concluded that "there is more substance than ceremony in the schedule of the vice-president." And the *New York Times,* after a study of the Mondale vice-presidency by Washing-

Once a week, when they were both in town, Mondale lunched with President Carter, and occasionally they were joined by a cabinet member. On this day, early in 1977, Energy Secretary John Schlesinger lunches with them to discuss energy problems facing the country.

ton correspondent Martin Tolchin, stated that Vice-President Mondale "wields more power than any other vice-president in recent history."

When Walter Mondale assumed the office of vice-president, he had some ideas of his own about the vice-presidency. "I decided to recommend to the president," he told a *National Journal* reporter, "that I not be assigned to [organizational] line functions," such as a special committee to examine problems in the welfare system. Mondale felt that most of the functions would, if they were significant, be already assigned to some cabinet or key executive officer and if they were not significant they would trivialize the vice-presidency. "I think, in the past," he adds, "vice-presidents have often taken on minor functions in order to make it appear that their role was significant when, if they were president, they wouldn't touch them at all. I decided to

Vice-President Mondale presides at a meeting of a special economic task force in the White House. Patricia Harris, secretary of Housing and Urban Development, is on his right.

stay away from that. . . . Secondly, I don't have the staff to run a major . . . function. Nor should I. It takes a lot of time away from your advisory role. The way it is now, I don't have to defend a bureaucratic office. And that's good. I can spend my time elsewhere. . . ."

The role Mondale preferred was that of an adviser to the president. "I see my role as a general adviser on almost any issue," he said, "as a trouble-shooter, as a representative of the president in certain foreign affairs matters, and as a political advocate of the administration." But he added: "My political influence is of a different nature. It's personal to the president. I am not a substitute or a deputy president."

The "Mondale model," as George Bush calls the active approach to the vice-presidency, appears to have set the mold for the modern

Vice-President Mondale lunches in the White House with a delegation from the liaison office of the People's Republic of China—before the United States established normal relations with Red China.

When he was in office, the vice-president took many trips abroad—to Western Europe and Japan, Portugal, Spain, Austria, London, South Africa, Canada, Mexico, Israel, Egypt, Italy, and Southeast Asia. Often a large press entourage traveled with him, affording an excellent opportunity for press conferences. En route to Brussels in 1977, Mondale talks with reporters David Broder (in dark suit), Herb Kaplow, Mel Elfin, and Cherle Avardson.

President Carter welcomes Vice-President and Mrs. Mondale as they return from their trip to Western Europe and Japan in early 1977.

Vice-President and Mrs. Bush were the first to greet the Americans held hostage in Iran when they arrived at Andrews Air Force Base for their White House reception.

Cynthia Johnson/The White House

office, defining its influence, powers, and limitations. With all his increased responsibilities, the vice-president can never be a "deputy president," as Gerald Ford discovered at the Republican convention in 1980. Having held the office of the presidency for more than two years, Gerald Ford, when approached by Ronald Reagan's men about the possibility of serving as Reagan's running mate in the presidential campaign of 1980, demanded that the job be elevated even more than it had been under Vice-President Mondale. He wanted the right to name some key men to the Reagan administration and other powers that would have given him the status of "copresident," as it was described in the press. Reagan declined and, instead, chose George Bush as his running mate.

When Bush assumed the vice-presidency in 1981, he immediately declared that the "Mondale model" seemed ideal to him and that he would attempt to emulate his predecessor's approach to the office. This, however, might not be possible because the activities and responsibilities of a vice-president are subject to the president's wishes. And there was considerable evidence that Ronald Reagan, who campaigned on the pledge to return America to its traditional values, probably had a traditional concept of the vice-presidency. Although Bush was given an office in the White House near the president's and was asked to sit in on the early Cabinet meetings, Reagan did not appear as eager to utilize his vice-president as Carter did. He indicated that Bush would be given responsibilities in foreign affairs and national security and in dealing with Congress, but he also stressed that he would be assigned many of the ceremonial duties that fall on the president—and that were the principal function of the traditional "Throttlebottom" vice-presidents. Reagan also told one reporter, prior to his election, that having the vice-president meet regularly with the Cabinet would be a waste of Bush's talents.

In the early months of the Reagan administration, Bush's role in the White House was sharply defined. Indeed, perhaps the most signifi-

Vice-President Bush (fourth from right at table) sits across from President Reagan (second from left) as he attends a cabinet meeting.   *Cynthia Johnson/The White House*

George Bush (left), with Ronald Reagan, waves to delegates at the 1980 Republican convention in Detroit, after Reagan had announced that Bush would be his running mate. As vice-president, Bush is given special attention by the press and the public because he is next to succeed the oldest American president ever to take office.

The Office of the Vice-Presidency

cant development in the role of the vice-president was President Reagan's decision to put Bush in charge of his administration's National Security Crisis Management team. It was an assignment that Zbigniew Brzezinski held in the Carter Administration and is an unprecedented responsibility for a vice-president.

Bush was called upon to act as a crisis manager much sooner than anyone thought possible, following the shocking assassination attempt on President Reagan in March of 1981. Bush was in Texas when the shooting occurred on a Monday afternoon, and Secretary of State Alexander Haig temporarily took command in the White House. But by that evening, the vice-president was in Washington working closely with the recuperating president to make certain that the government of the United States continued to function.

The Fringe Benefits

The Constitution does not mention wages for the vice-president. However, the First Congress agreed that the vice-president should have an annual salary and granted him $5,000 a year. Today, the vice-president is allowed $79,125 a year, plus $10,000 for operating and entertainment expenses. He has a staff of more than forty and, since Nelson Rockefeller's term of office, is given a free residence in the old Naval Observatory on Massachusetts Avenue, which is maintained by the navy. He also has a limousine—provided by the Secret Service—and the use of U.S. Air Force planes for travel.

The vice-president is the only government official to have four offices. His formal office is in Room 274 of the Executive Office Building, adjacent to the White House. He also has an office near the president's in the White House. He has another office in the Capitol and one in the Dirksen Senate Office Building. Most of the time, however, Bush, like Mondale before him, works in his White House office.

Vice-President Harry S. Truman speaks for a cancer program in April 1945. This is thought to be the last photograph taken of Truman as vice-president.

6

"It Is the Man Who Makes the Office, Not the Office the Man"

Whatever our founding fathers and nineteenth-century political leaders might have thought of the vice-presidency, the office has come of age today. In the middle of the twentieth century, it is a powerful and responsible job, held in the highest respect by political leaders and foreign dignitaries. More and more it is sought after by aspiring politicians. Here a few men who have recently held the office give their thoughts on the vice-presidency.

"It has always been my feeling that this office, which is the second highest honor that can be bestowed by the American people, has great inherent and potential dignity that has been sadly neglected. The opportunities afforded by the vice-presidency, particularly the presidency of the Senate, do not come—they are there to be seized. The man who fills the office can choose to do little or he can do much. The vice-president's influence on legislation depends on his personality and his ability, and especially the respect which he commands from the senators. Here is one instance in which it is the man who makes the office, not the office the man."

—Harry S. Truman

155

"I felt that [the vice-presidency] offered opportunities that I had really never had before, in either my service in the House or the Senate. I . . . never felt the vice-presidency was a comedown from anything except the presidency. . . ."

—Lyndon B. Johnson

The Lyndon B. Johnson Library

". . . It is important for a vice-president to remember that he is not the president and, therefore, can only speak for the government when he is authorized to do so. I believe it is important for the vice-president to be loyal to the president's policies and at the same time to speak candidly, in private, with the president in any disagreements in policy, so that the president may have the benefit of the vice-president's advice and counsel. . . . I emphasize the personal relationship. It isn't good enough to convey one's observations to the president's subordinates."

—Hubert H. Humphrey

"Having little use for kings, our founding fathers knew nonetheless that that monarch's main virtue is assured continuity. The Roman republic, which was the best model they had in 1787, was at last brought down by civil struggles over successions. . . .

"Every vice-presidency in my memory has been as different as the vice-presidents I have known: Truman, Barkley, Nixon, Johnson, Humphrey, Agnew. Among the variables are the degree of intimacy, past and present, between a president and vice-president; their respective styles and attitudes; their relative rapport with Congress and the news media; the particular strengths and political skills which a vice-president can contribute to the administration team; and such independent constituencies as each may have in their party or country as a whole."

—Gerald R. Ford

Shortly after becoming president, Gerald Ford waves to people on the street as he rides in the presidential limousine. The memorandum in his left hand is from Secretary of State Henry Kissinger, and it reads: "I enclose a list of the foreign leaders to whom you sent messages on the assumption of the presidency and a summary of the responses that have been received." *The White House*

"The president is overwhelmed and, if you're not careful, could be literally paralyzed by the minutiae of government detail. And the trick, it seems to me, is to make certain the president has time to spend on the fundamental issues that affect us at home and abroad— issues like working toward a fully employed, noninflationary economy, an economy that is efficient, fair, and equitable; making sure government works well and responsively; trying to reduce international tensions, strategic arms, and the rest.

"These are the great issues that affect mankind, affect American citizens in the most direct and profound way. And the president's time ought to be primarily spent pondering, understanding, and dealing with those issues. That's where I think I can help the president the most."

—Walter F. Mondale

159

The Office of the Vice-Presidency

" My role, as the president has stated publicly, will be in dealing with the Congress, with national security, and foreign policy. What is important, however, is my relationship with President Reagan. The duties, responsibilities, and influence of the vice-president, at least in my thinking, will flow from the president in terms measured by his confidence in me.

"I will be a vice-president who is loyal to the president, one who will offer advice and council based on my experience in past government positions, and my current knowledge of issues, and this will be given to him in confidence and kept in confidence."

—George Bush

Index

Page numbers in *italics* refer to illustrations

161

164

Stalin, Joseph, *37*
Stamp Act, 13
Stassen, Harold, *5*
Stevenson, Adlai E. (grandfather), 82–83, *82*
Stevenson, Adlai E. (grandson), 37, 39, 82, *82*
Stuart, Jeb, 69
Summerfield, Arthur E., *5*
Supreme Court, Roosevelt's attempt to "pack," 43, 98–99

Taft, William Howard, 30, 87, 89
Tariff Act of 1846, 65
Taylor, Zachary, 17, 21
Tecumseh, 63
"Throttlebottom, Alexander," 96, 151
Thurmond, J. Strom, 37
Tilden, Samuel, 77, 79
"Tippecanoe and Tyler Too," 19
Tolchin, Martin, 147
Tompkins, Daniel D., *58, 59*
Truman, Bess, *4*
Truman, Harry S., *x*, 2, *4, 8*, 34–37, *34*, 101, 103, 106, *134*, 135, *154*
    quoted, 49, 121, 133, 155
Truman, Margaret, *4*
Truman Doctrine, 36
"Tweed gang," 25
Tydings, Joseph R., 142
Tyler, John, 2, 18–19, *18*, 61, 67, 126

Van Buren, Martin, 16–17, *16*, 63, 65, 131
"Veep," 103
vice-presidency
    cabinet meetings and, *5*, 33, 93, 103, 131, 151
    development of, 123–36
    duties of, 1, *3, 5, 6*, 8, 23
    importance of, 2–8, 44–45, 85, 101, 103, 107, 116

vice-presidency *(continued)*
    as insignificant office, 1–2, 11, 30, 49–50, 83, 96, 120–21
    modern, 146–53
    "Mondale model" of, *145*, 148, 151
    National Security Council and, 103, 135
    salary for, 153
    senatorial role of, 1, 36
    statistics on, 2, 8, 13, 38, 47, 55, 56, 60, 66, 68, 89, 93, 95, 102, 109, 120, 126, 131
    thoughts on, 155–60
    vacancies in, 61, 67
Vietnam War, 40, 45, 107
Virginia, University of, 15

Wallace, Henry A., 36, 37, 99, 100–101, *100*, 133, *134*
Wallace, Henry C., 100–101
"War Hawks," 61
War of 1812, 59, 61, 63, 65
Warren, Charles, 94
Washington, George, 12, 13, 123, 131
Watergate affair, *7*, 41, 119, 135
Weed, Thurlow, 21
Weeks, Sinclair, *5*
Wheeler, William A., *76*, 77
Whig party, 19, 21, 75
whistle stops, in campaign of 1948, 103
Wilmot Proviso, 75
Wilson, Charles E., *5*
Wilson, Edith, 127
Wilson, Henry, 74–75, *74*
Wilson, Woodrow, 11, 31, 49, 89, 91, 127, 131
World War I, 35, 93
World War II, 36, 43–44, 46, 101, 110, 132–33
Wright, Silas, 120

Young, Philip, *5*

Roy Hoopes was born in Salt Lake City, Utah, but grew up in Washington, D.C. He earned his bachelor's and master's degrees at George Washington University in Washington. During World War II, he served as a communications and deck officer on an LST in the South Pacific. Since the war, Mr. Hoopes has worked for the State Department, the Department of Health, Education and Welfare, and a number of newspapers and magazines, including *Time-Life International, The Washingtonian,* and the *National Geographic.*

He is the author of twenty-one books, including *Getting with Politics, The Peace Corps Experience,* and *Americans Remember the Homefront.* This is his eighth book of photographic studies for young adults, which include *What the President of the United States Does, What a United States Senator Does,* and *What a Pro Football Coach Does.* He has recently completed a biography of the American novelist James M. Cain. He lives in Washington, D.C., with his wife and one son.

920
HOO

Hoopes, Roy

The changing vice-
presidency

$15.00 C.1

DATE		
MAR 0 7 1984		
MAR. 23 1984		
MAR. 21 1988		
FEB. 1 0 1994		

© THE BAKER & TAYLOR CO.